THE FAKE FOOD COOKBOOK

The Fake Food Cookbook: Props You Can't Eat for Theatre, Film, and TV contains step-by-step instructions on how to create the most realistic prop food for a theatrical production. From appetizers such as oysters on a half shell and chicken wings, entrées such as lobster and honey-glazed ham, to desserts, breakfasts, and even beverages, every meal is covered in this how-to guide. Full color images of each step and finished products illustrate each recipe, along with suggestions for keeping the budget for each project low. Safety Data Sheets and links to informative videos are hosted on a companion website.

Karestin Harrison is currently the Technical Theatre Director at Cardinal Gibbons High School, in Raleigh, NC. She has worked in the art department on two feature films in roles as set dresser for *Susie's Hope* and set decorator for *The Ultimate Life*. Karestin has been a props artisan at several regional theatres including PlayMakers Repertory Company, North Carolina Theatre, Utah Shakespeare Festival, and Cincinnati Playhouse in the Park.

Tamara L. Honesty is the Assistant Professor of Scenic Design at Kent State University. Tammy is a member of USA Local 829 as a scenic designer and has been a professional scenic artist for River City Scenic and at 3dx Scenic Studio where she was also a project manager. Examples of her painting talents have cruised the world on Royal Caribbean Cruise Lines, Princess Cruises, and Norwegian Cruise Lines. She has been a prop master at Cornell University, the Human Race Theatre Company, and for many university productions. Tammy is a member and on the Board of Directors of USITT, as well as the Programming Coordinator for USITT's Annual Conference & Stage Expo.

THE FAKE FOOD COOKBOOK

PROPS YOU CAN'T EAT FOR THEATRE, FILM, AND TV

**KARESTIN HARRISON
TAMARA L. HONESTY**

First published 2018
by Routledge
711 Third Avenue, New York, NY 10017

and by Routledge
2 Park Square, Milton Park, Abingdon, Oxon, OX14 4RN

Routledge is an imprint of the Taylor & Francis Group, an informa business

© 2018 Taylor & Francis

The right of Karestin Harrison and Tamara L. Honesty to be identified as authors of this work has been asserted by them in accordance with sections 77 and 78 of the Copyright, Designs and Patents Act 1988.

All rights reserved. No part of this book may be reprinted or reproduced or utilised in any form or by any electronic, mechanical, or other means, now known or hereafter invented, including photocopying and recording, or in any information storage or retrieval system, without permission in writing from the publishers.

Trademark notice: Product or corporate names may be trademarks or registered trademarks, and are used only for identification and explanation without intent to infringe.

Library of Congress Cataloging-in-Publication Data
A catalog record for this title has been requested.

ISBN: 978-1-138-50557-5 (hbk)
ISBN: 978-1-138-21227-5 (pbk)
ISBN: 978-1-315-45081-0 (ebk)

Typeset in Univers
by Saxon Graphics Ltd, Derby

Visit the companion website: www.routledge.com/cw/honesty

Printed and bound in India by Replika Press Pvt. Ltd.

contents

Acknowledgments vii
Preface ix

Section 1 introduction **1**

Chapter 1   why make fake food? 3

Chapter 2   tools and safety 6

Chapter 3   salt dough recipes 20

Section 2 appetizers **23**

Chapter 4   bread: baguette, round sourdough bread, half loaf of a rustic
            round, and rye loaf 25

Chapter 5   cheese platter: brie, cheddar, swiss, and gouda 32

Chapter 6   chicken wings 37

Chapter 7   egg rolls, spring rolls, and soy sauce 42

Chapter 8   oysters on the half shell 47

Chapter 9   popcorn 50

Chapter 10 shrimp cocktail 54

Chapter 11 vegetable tray 59

Chapter 12 wonton soup 64

Section 3 breakfast food **69**

Chapter 13 doughnuts 71

Chapter 14 oatmeal muffins 76

Chapter 15 pancake, bacon, and egg breakfast 79

Chapter 16 sticky buns 85

Section 4	**main entrées and side dishes**	**91**
Chapter 17	baked potato with butter and sour cream	93
Chapter 18	barbecue ribs with corn on the cob	99
Chapter 19	chef salad	106
Chapter 20	chicken lo mein	112
Chapter 21	club sandwich	117
Chapter 22	hanging meats	123
Chapter 23	honey-glazed ham	129
Chapter 24	lettuce wraps	133
Chapter 25	lobster tail	137
Chapter 26	pierogi	141
Chapter 27	roast beef with mashed potatoes and gravy	144
Chapter 28	salmon fillet with side salad	148
Chapter 29	spinach quiche	152
Chapter 30	turkey	156
Section 5	**beverages**	**163**
Chapter 31	beer	165
Chapter 32	hot chocolate	168
Chapter 33	irish coffee	171

Chapter 34	lemonade	174
Chapter 35	martini with olives	177
Chapter 36	milk: white and chocolate	181
Chapter 37	piña colada	184
Section 6	**desserts**	**187**
Chapter 38	apple tart	189
Chapter 39	cake with removable piece	194
Chapter 40	cherry pie	201
Chapter 41	chocolate cake à la mode	205
Chapter 42	coconut cream pie	210
Chapter 43	gelatin mold	214
Chapter 44	pineapple upside-down cake	218
	companion website information	223
	helpful resources	224
	products used	225
	bibliography	226
	Index	227

Acknowledgments

We would like to express our gratitude to Joel Svendsen, Jenny Knott, and fellow employees at Rosco® for their support on this book and allowing us to experiment with so many of their wonderful products.

Our heartfelt thanks go to Debra Hildebrand for sharing her recipes for edible beverages, food, and blood that she has concocted throughout her career at Cincinnati Playhouse in the Park.

We would like to thank Stacey Walker who championed this proposal to her coworkers at Routledge. She was excited about this project since the idea came about five years ago and again last spring when it became a reality. We would like to thank Meredith Darnell, and Mhairi Bennett, both of whom have answered our endless questions every step of the way. We would like to extend our appreciation to all at Routledge for taking a chance on us and sharing our belief that a book about fake food was needed.

the craft of creating fake food. I would like to thank my teachers at both Greensboro College and College-Conservatory of Music, University of Cincinnati, especially John Saari, Brian Ruggaber, and Stirling Shelton.

My dearest compliments go out to all the people I have worked with over the years; your work inspires me and helps push me to create the best food possible.

Thanks to my sous chefs at Cardinal Gibbons who helped get dishes to the finished product. I must thank friends, Brittany, Katie, Kim, and Amy who have constantly supported me, given feedback, and provided encouragement when I felt I couldn't get the book accomplished.

I would like to thank my parents, first for being my parents but also for believing in me when I said I wanted to do theatre so many years ago. Thanks to my family who have been cheerleaders since day one.

Special Thanks from Karestin Harrision

This book would not have happened without the endless support and encouragement of my fiancé, Lucas Johnson.

I must give thanks to my fellow author, Tammy Honesty, who tirelessly cheered on my work from graduate school till now. Without her support and push this book wouldn't have happened. She took my simple recipes and turned them into something concrete. I had the opportunity to create the dishes, while she did the heavy lifting on preparing the book- I will forever be grateful for her.

Thanks must go out to all the bosses I have had throughout my career: Ben Hohman, Kristina Stevenson, and Jason Curtis who have all given me the opportunity and support to explore

Special Thanks from Tamara L. Honesty

To my husband, Chuck Hatcher, whose constant love, support, and encouragement helped make this project possible. Not only did he urge me to find a way to make this dream a reality, but also he helped by editing, shopping, and taking photographs. I could not have accomplished all that I have without his help.

Thank you to my co-author and partner in crime, Karestin Harrison. It was a joy to collaborate on a project again with her. I have always enjoyed working with her from our first project when I designed the set for *Picnic* and she created beautiful props, crab grass, and bare patches for the show and throughout this project. Thank you for answering countless texts and emails over the past year.

Thank you to Mary McClung who inspired and showed me that it was possible to write a book. And thanks to my friends Julia, Stirling, Steve, Cary, and Patrick for their support and encouragement.

This book would not exist without the year I was teaching at the University of Cincinnati-CCM, working with Brian Ruggaber and Kat Miller as we helped shepherd Karestin through her final research project. Their knowledge and expertise was a key component of the original project. Not to mention the support from the faculty, staff, and students of the Department of Theatre Design & Production.

If not for my involvement with USITT, I don't think this book would exist. The opportunity to meet people like Jenny Knott, Stacey Walker, and Joel Svendsen who could help turn this idea into a reality was essential.

I would be amiss if I didn't express my gratitude for the support for this project given to me by my colleagues and students at Kent State University School of Theatre & Dance. I wish to thank Terry Martin who spent a day with me as a "proptender" recreating the edible beverages.

Thank you to the countless props artisans who shared their ideas and expertise.

Finally, I would like to my family: Lani, Shelley, Terry, Holly, George, Drew, and Mason for always supporting my passion and love of theatre that has turned into a career.

preface

The first iteration of this cookbook began with Karestin's passion for creating a collection of 25 fake food recipes for her MFA final research project at the University of Cincinnati-CCM. Her thesis was to illustrate the benefits of creating artificial dishes rather than of using actual food. From those original 25 recipes, we expanded to include more dishes that are commonly seen in the entertainment industry.

Making fake food is similar to real cooking because both are experimental and recipes can be modified to suit personal taste. The format of this book emulates traditional cookbooks found in most kitchens, showing the step-by-step creation of a variety of simulated food items including meats, breakfast foods, drinks, desserts, and more. The book will give you a glimpse into the vast array of materials and techniques that can be used to create dishes. Materials include items that can be found at local stores or from online distributors. We include materials that range from inexpensive to moderately expensive to show a variety of options. The materials used in this book are not the only ones available. Likewise, the techniques seen in this book are not the only way to create these recipes, but can serve as a starting place for developing other approaches. In the world of prop making, there is no one "right" way to build anything. You may discover an entirely different way to achieve these recipes. Please reach out to us if you find a product or a technique that works better. We are all better artisans when we collaborate and learn from each other.

This cookbook assumes the reader has a basic knowledge of mold-making and casting techniques. For more extensive information on casting and mold making check out the Smooth-On® website (www.smooth-on.com) or Eric Hart's book The Prop Building Guidebook: For Theatre, Film, and TV. Smooth-On® products were used exclusively for mold making and casting in this book because of personal preference. Smooth-On® products have readily available trial kits at local art and craft supply stores. A trial kit will make one or more projects, the quality of the product is excellent, and most products do not require a scale to accurately measure Part A and Part B before mixing.

No fake food cookbook could be completely comprehensive or include all of the numerous dishes required for all productions. The recipes in this book have been limited to items that are based on shows we, or our prop artisan friends, have done that needed fake food.

Our hope is that by using this book you will gain experience utilizing a range of techniques and a variety of materials to apply to your next fake food "cooking" adventure.

Section 1
introduction

one

why make fake food?

The question of why create fake food instead of using real food for props is frequently asked. The answer is not cut and dry. There are several advantages to creating fake food including cost, storage, and reusability. Depending on the length of the run, creating fake food could be beneficial. If a production is scheduled to run for weeks at a regional theater or months on Broadway, creating fake food could be the most cost and time effective. It would cost far less to create the dish or dishes once then reuse them, than buy perishable items every night. By making the fake food from scratch, there is more flexibility and creativity in what the final piece looks like instead of buying them commercially manufactured. It is much easier to tweak the coloring or shape during the creation as opposed to altering a mass-produced item.

However, edible food does have several benefits in certain situations: if the show has a very short run, the actors must consume the food as part of the action on stage, or there is an extremely limited construction time for props. Limited time for build, labor, or for the entire production run may make having real food or some variation of real food more practical, especially for drinks.

On the other hand, creating fake food can be an exciting project for anyone of any skill level who has the desire to experiment and explore the possibilities. Before beginning any project, first research what the real food looks like—either buy an actual item at the grocery store or find photos on the internet. The research is essential to the creation of a prop that looks realistic in color, shape, texture, and sheen.

The recipes in this book help show how simple products found at hardware, grocery, and craft stores can be used in creating good-looking dishes for a fraction of the cost of buying commercially made fake food. Many of the products used were under $20 and were used for several of the dishes. These products are beneficial for educational, community, and smaller theaters with limited budget and supplies. Some of the more expensive products such as Smooth-On® OOMOO® or Smooth-Cast® only used trial-size kits that are around $30. Often one trial-size kit was utilized to make multiple dishes. The more expensive coatings or adhesives like Rosco® CrystalGel, Rosco® FoamCoat, or Sculptural Art Coating's Sculpt or Coat® are formulated to work on a variety of materials. Although the initial cost is higher, the quality and the success balance out the initial upfront cost. The Rosco® Scenic Paint Test Kit or Sculptural Art Coating's Artist's Choice™ Paint Starter Kit are available from vendors like Rosebrand® or Production Advantage. The kits contain 1 oz. samples and cost between $70 and $85 depending on the vendor. The kits are available for Rosco® Off Broadway™ or Rosco® Supersaturated™ product lines. One kit will be able to create almost all of the recipes in this book.

Fake food is also more durable than real food and can be preserved for years by storing it in plastic storage bags and bins. First, the item should be completely dry. Then, place in a zippered storage bag, remove all the air from the bag, and seal the bag. Place the bag in a plastic storage bin with a tight-fitting lid. If the fake food is stored correctly, it can be saved and reused year after year. For example, for the annual production of *A Christmas Carol* that requires a roasted goose and other items for the feast, all of those items could be pulled from storage and perhaps only need a little bit of freshening up before they are ready for a performance. Several of the dishes do take several hours or even days to fully complete and while it may seem easier to just buy/make real food, in the long run you are saving money and the time the crew has to spend cooking food if it is purely set dressing or if the actors mime eating it.

Another example is for Stage One's touring production of *The Diary of Anne Frank* from Kelly Wiegant Mangan. In the show, the characters spend one scene snapping green beans for cooking. The budget wouldn't allow for fresh beans for each performance and the touring crew wouldn't have enough time to get fresh green beans. They cast the green bean out of green wax. The cast wax beans had a great sound when they were snapped and the pieces could be recycled into the next batch. The crew traveled with several molds and a toaster oven. Only when they were at a venue for two days or more would they recast the beans. It was an extremely simple and cheap alternative.

If the items need to sit out for long periods on a film or photo shoot, then artificial food might be a more viable solution. Real food may spoil and attract insects. Fake food would also provide continuity throughout the day or from one day to the next.

Fake food can be repurposed from one project to another. The food created for a photo shoot could end up in a stage production. Or the same food items could be used for different stage productions. For example, breakfast food created for *The Spitfire Grill* could be used in other shows like the Sheryl Crow/Barry Levinson new musical *Diner*, William Inge's *Bus Stop*, or the Sara Bareilles/Jessie Nelson musical *Waitress*. The roasted turkey and goose could be in several productions including Dickens's *A Christmas Carol*, Kaufman and Hart's *You Can't Take It with You*, or any opera or play calling for a feast on stage. William Inge's play *Picnic* calls for several different items including pies, deviled eggs, and chicken.

There are a wide variety of materials and techniques an artisan gets to experiment with when creating artificial food. A few of the materials that can be used to make fake food are foam, Play-doh®, ribbon, wood, glue, shellacs, candle waxes, paint, and thermoplastics. Creating fake food also provides the opportunity to explore casting and mold making. Smooth-On® has several excellent step-by-step video tutorials on casting and mold making ranging from the *Basics of Mold Making* to *Advanced Techniques*, using all the different series of products including OOMOO®, Smooth-Cast®, Dragon Skin®, FOAM-iT!®, and FlexFoam-iT!®. Links to videos can be found on their website at www.smooth-on.com/tutorials/. Rosco® has a blog dedicated to showcasing tutorials and articles on how customers have used their products; it can be found at www.rosco.com/spectrum/. It is a great resource because it is searchable by typing in the product name and various blog posts will appear that can give you information and ideas for how the product may work for your project.

two

tools and safety

Preparing to make fake food is a little like baking or cooking: you need to gather the necessary tools and ingredients. Most items fall within three categories: basic, intermediate, and advanced. Many recipes for projects in this book can be accomplished by using objects found in the basic tool and product section. They can be found at the grocery store or the local craft store such as Michael's®, Hobby Lobby®, Walmart®, Jo-Ann Fabrics & Craft Stores®, or A.C. Moore Arts & Crafts®. The intermediate section includes tools and products found at hardware stores or craft stores and a few specialty items found online. The advanced section has items available at theatrical supply vendors, specialty hardware, or woodworking stores. Specific trademarked products are cited because they are the products used in the recipes. There are many similar products by different manufacturers that may be cheaper or more expensive and perform just as well as the products listed in this chapter and in the recipes. *Not all products used in all the recipes are included in this list.*

Basic Tools and Products

- **Measuring Tools:**
  - **12" or 18" Ruler:** A plastic ruler will suffice; however, a metal ruler with a cork back is preferable. The 12" or 18" metal ruler is one of the most essential tools because in addition to a measuring device, it can also serve as a cutting utensil when working with clay or Crayola® Model Magic®.
  - **Tape Measure:** A steel tape measure is a staple for measuring. One that has a good locking feature is especially helpful to make accurate measurements.
  - **Cloth Measuring Tape:** A flexible cloth measuring tape is helpful to accurately measure curved or flat surfaces.
  - **Measuring Cups:** Either glass or plastic measuring cups can be used to accurately measure ingredients. If the measuring cups have been used for creating fake food, they should be labeled as such and should never be used again for cooking edible food items.

- **Marking Utensils:**
  - **Pencil:** The pencil is the most useful, underrated, and often most scarce item in a shop.
  - **Sharpie® Marker:** Sharpie® Markers use indelible ink and comes in a wide variety of colors.
- **Cutting Tools:**
  - **X-acto® Knife:** An X-acto® knife is a precision cutting tool with a handle and a clamping mechanism that tightens on a variety of blade types. An X-acto® knife is key when cutting pieces of paper, modeling clay, or shaving off excess material from projects. The #11 blade is the most frequently used. When the blade dulls, the blade should be changed. Dispose of the used blades by either depositing them in a sharps disposal container or taping around all edges of the blade before placing in a trashcan.

Figure 2.1A: X-acto® knife set

8   introduction

Figure 2.1B: Metal ruler (top), Snap-off blade knife, scissors, and #11 X-acto® knife on a cutting mat

- ○ **Scissors:** All-purpose scissors are the most useful; however, when cutting fabric, scissors only used on fabric are helpful to create clean cuts.
- ○ **Utility Knife or Snap-Off Blade Knife:** The utility knife, also commonly called a mat knife or box cutter, is an all-purpose cutting tool. The snap-off blade knife is also known as a box cutter. There are two advantages the snap-off blade knife has over its cousin, the utility knife. The first is as the point of the blade dulls, pliers can be used to snap off sections of the blade creating a new sharp, albeit shorter, blade. The second advantage is that the blade can be extended to its full length to carve foam. Other knives can also be used to cut foam. Standard steak knives are another essential tool for carving foam because they have a long, sharp blade with more rigidity than a snap-off blade.

- **Self-Healing Cutting Mat**—(various sizes—most useful are 11" x 17" and 24" x 36"): A self-healing cutting mat protects your work surface, helps keep the X-acto® blade (or any knife blade, for that matter) from dulling as quickly, and the gridlines aid with measuring and cutting fabric, paper, and modeling materials.
- **Crayons:** A cheap package of crayons can be used for tinting cream or gel candle wax.
- **Modeling Clay or Dough:**
  - ○ **Crayola® Model Magic®:** Crayola® Model Magic® is readily available at craft stores and discount stores like Walmart® and Target®. It is extremely easy to use, air-dries fairly quickly, is paintable, and comes in a wide variety of colors. According to the company website, it remains somewhat flexible when dry. Typically, it takes about 3 hours for it to dry enough to paint. The website also states it takes 24–72 hours to dry completely.
  - ○ **Salt Dough:** Salt dough is an extremely inexpensive method to make modeling clay from household items (flour, salt, vegetable oil, alum or cream of tartar, and water). After mixing the items together, they will keep for a few days in an airtight container. It has to be baked to harden the dough.
- **Adhesives:**
  - ○ **Hot Glue Gun:** A hot glue gun is helpful when attaching various materials together. It is important to keep in mind that hot glue is considered a temporary adhesive. Also, remember hot glue guns get extremely hot and can cause first-, second-, or even third-degree burns if not used carefully. Always make sure to have something underneath the tip of the gun to protect your work surface, as the glue will melt anything in its path. Hot glue comes in low-temp or high-temp varieties referring to the temperature at which the glue melts.
  - ○ **Elmer's® Glue-All®:** Known affectionately as Elmer's® or "white glue," this is a water-based flexible adhesive that dries clear and can be found at craft and discount stores in small quantities or at hardware stores in gallon

containers. There are many companies that make similar white flexible glue including Titebond®, Techno Adhesives Co., Rosebrand®, and Rosco®.

- **Acrylic Paints:** Acrylic or any water-based paint in a variety of colors is necessary for many of the project recipes. If you have black, white, and the three primary colors (red, yellow, blue), and a good understanding of how pigment color theory works, you will be able to mix any color you need. There is an excellent YouTube video on color theory at www.youtube.com/watch?v=WYZWDEmLR90. Paint can be artist paint in tubes or bottles from the craft store or it can be house paint from the hardware store which can be cheaper than the high-quality, yet more expensive scenic products from Rosco® or Sculptural Arts®.

- **Various Sizes of Brushes–Chip and Detail Brushes:** Paint brushes in an assortment of sizes are helpful for accuracy and execution. Chip brushes are inexpensive pure bristle brushes that come in sizes ranging from ½" to 4" priced from 30¢ to $4. A basic variety pack of artist's detail brushes can be purchased at a local craft store for under $20.

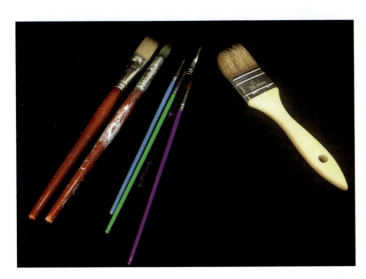

Figure 2.2: Detail brushes and chip brush

- **Sandpaper—80, 150, and 220 Grit:** Sandpaper is useful for smoothing out edges of foam or wood. It is classified by grit. The smaller the number like 60 or 80, the coarser the sandpaper is. The larger the number like 150 or 220, the finer the texture of the sandpaper. The finer sandpaper such as 220 is designed to do fine detail work.
- **Wax Paper:** Wax paper is handy for keeping the cutting mat and working areas clean.
- **Clear Plastic Wrap:** Plastic wrap is a good covering for conserving paints and a way to section off the fake food from consumable portions, if you using edible with inedible food in the same dish.
- **Q-tips® Cotton Swabs:** Cotton swabs are readily available, useful for mixing paints, and for painting on small objects.
- **Paper Products:**
  - **Bounty® Paper Towels:** Paper towels are helpful for cleaning up spills and have an interesting texture that can be utilized for creating lettuce or other leafy vegetation. Bounty® was chosen for its texture.
  - **Cottonelle® Toilet Paper:** Cottonelle® Toilet Paper has a texture that is useful for creating lettuce or other leafy vegetation.
- **Mixing Containers:** Mixing containers like 8-ounce clear plastic cups (like Solo® or Dixie® brand) are handy because they are disposable; they have ridges that are useful when measuring two-part components for Smooth-On® products; and a Sharpie® will easily mark levels to accurately measure the separate components.
- **Saucepan:** A small saucepan is necessary for melting candle wax. A saucepan that has been used to melt wax should never be used again for cooking edible food items. It should be labeled in some way, like "wax only," so there is no confusion with a pan that can be used for consumable foods.
- **Mixing Tools:**
  - **Spatulas, Spoons, Tongue Depressors/Jumbo Wooden Craft Sticks:** Spoons and spatulas used for creating fake food should never be used again for

Figure 2.3: Icing spatula

Figure 2.4: Japanese Ryoba pull saw

cooking edible food items. Make sure these are either in a labeled container or are labeled individually so there is no cross-contamination with real food prep tools. Tongue depressors or jumbo wooden craft sticks are inexpensive and disposable.
- **Cheese Grater:** A cheese grater is an excellent tool used with waxes to create shredded cheese or a little bit of zest on a dish. If a cheese grater is used for creating fake food it should never be used again for cooking edible food items and should be labeled or kept in a separate storage place to avoid contaminating edible food.
- **Tweezers:** Tweezers are a tool that can come in very handy when trying to put tiny beads to represent seeds on to a dish such as kiwi or poppy seed muffins.

Intermediate Tools and Products

- **Cutting and Shaping Tools:**
  - **Japanese Ryoba Hand Saw:** Often referred to as simply a "Japanese Saw." It is a multi-purpose type of handsaw that cuts on a pull stroke and has two cutting edges. It is useful for trimming items flush and for cutting a rough shape in foam. It is a good alternative to using a band saw.
  - **Orbital Sander:** An orbital sander is also known as a palm sander (because it fits in the palm of your hand) or quarter-sheet sander (because it uses one-quarter of a sheet of sand paper). The orbital sander is a step up from regular sandpaper. It is powered by an electric motor and provides the benefit of more sanding and shaping in less time.
  - **Jig Saw or Sabre Saw:** The jig saw and the sabre saw are synonymous terms for a handheld small blade reciprocating saw. It can be used to cut wood, plastic, and foam less than 3" in thickness. Be sure you are using the correct blade for the type of material to be cut. Before cutting, always clamp the piece to a working surface or table.
  - **Rasp, Stanley® Surform® Shaver™ or Stanley® Pocket Plane™:** Often referred to simply as a Surform®, this tool looks like a small 2½" cheese grater on a handle. It is technically a rasp designed for woodworking that works on either a push or pull stroke. It can also be used to shape foam and to distress fabric.
  - **Cookie Cutters:** Metal cookie cutters, of all shapes, are helpful when cutting out salt dough, clay, or foam; or for making templates on paper, fabric, or wood.
  - **Clamps:** There are two types of clamps recommended for these projects. The C-clamp looks like the letter "C" and has a screw that closes the jaw. C-clamps with a 4" to 6" opening are the most useful. Bar clamps, like

Figure 2.5: Stanley® Surform® Shaver

Figure 2.6: Titebond® II Premium Wood Glue

the Quick Grip® manufactured by Irwin Tools®, are often more handy because the jaw slides on a bar allowing it to be tightened with one hand. It also features a trigger that tightens the jaw on to the item and it has a quick-release lever. Having several Quick Grip® clamps that are a minimum of 12" in length is beneficial. Remember when using any clamp on foam, the pressure of the clamp can dent the foam. It is a good practice to sandwich the foam to be laminated between two sheets of wood like lauan, Masonite, or plywood to help evenly distribute the pressure from the clamps.

- **Adhesives:**
  - **Titebond® Wood Glue:** Titebond® has a large selection of specific types of glues. Often referred to as simply "Titebond®" or "wood glue" or "yellow glue." Titebond® Wood Glue is different from Elmer's® Glue-All® because it provides a strong initial tacky surface and it cures faster which reduces the time the material needs to be clamped. Wood glue can also be used to laminate foam when applied liberally to the surface. It also creates a stronger bond between materials than Elmer's® Glue-All®. There are many companies that make wood glue including Elmer's®.
- **Measuring or Decorating Tools:**
  - **Cake Decorating Stand:** A cake decorating stand can help with the painting and finishing of food items since it has a plate that rotates.
  - **Candle Thermometer:** A candle thermometer is necessary to determine how hot wax is when it is in its liquid form. Generally, the candle wax used in these recipes should not be heated to more than 220°F.
  - **Adhesive Spreader:** This is a notched piece of metal used to spread adhesive for tiling projects, but it can be used to create a ribbed texture on fake frosting on cakes. There is an equivalent product made for edible cake decorating.

12 introduction

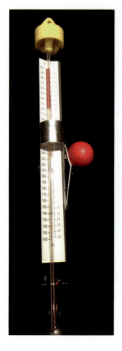

Figure 2.7: Candle wax thermometer

Figure 2.8: Adhesive spreader

- **Products:**
  - **Shellac:** Shellac is a resin that can be applied by brush as a colorant, glaze, wood finish, or a sealer. Zinsser® Bulls Eye® Shellac comes in both amber and clear. In most of the recipes where shellac is used, amber was chosen although it has no bearing on the outcome of its use. Shellac dries fast. It cleans up with denatured alcohol or ammonia and water, according to the Zinsser® website. Shellac is flammable and should be stored in a flammables cabinet.
  - **Candle Wax:** Yaley™ makes two types of candle-making materials used frequently in recipes in this book: Gel Wax® and Crème Wax®. Both of these waxes can be melted in a pot on the stovetop then poured into molds to become anything from corn on the cob to cheese to a hard-boiled egg. Both of these waxes are tintable with concentrated candle dye or, for the budget-minded, crayons. Projects like hot chocolate that used the Gel Wax® and Crème Wax® have lasted over five years and still look as good as the first day they were made.
  - **Polly Plastics™ Moldable Plastic Pellets:** Polly Plastics™ Moldable Plastic Pellets are easy to use. They melt in hot water (> 150ºF). They can be manipulated into any shape by hand or by tools. The pellets are clear, but Polly Plastics™ Color Pellets can be added to easily change the color. Both the Moldable Plastic Pellets and the Color Pellets are inexpensive and are available online and at some craft stores. A similar product is AMACO Friendly Plastic® Pellets, which are also available online and at local craft stores.
  - **India Ink:** India ink comes in about 24 different colors that are lightfast and permanent. India ink is mostly used for drawing or cartooning, but in the application of fake food it can be added to acrylic sealers, paints, and glue to create different sauces and finishes. Concentrated liquid watercolor, like Dr. Ph. Martin's®, will achieve a similar effect.
  - **Design Master® Spray Paint:** Design Master® has several product lines of aerosol tints, dyes, glazes, and sealers. The Colortool® line is safe on fresh flowers and Styrofoam™. Design Master® Glossy Wood Tone Spray often adds the finishing touch of creating a golden brown color of oven baking on baked goods and meat entrées.
  - **Flexible Polyurethane Foam (FPF):** Flexible polyurethane foam is commonly referred to as "upholstery foam" or "squishy foam." Often it is found in a white, yellowish-tan, or green color at a fabric store like Jo-Ann Fabric & Craft Store®. It can be painted, cut, carved, and glued. In several recipes, it is used to simulate bread because its texture and properties are similar.

tools and safety   **13**

○ **Rigid Extruded Polystyrene (XPS) Foam:** Rigid extruded polystyrene foam is more commonly referred to as pink or blue insulation foam. Several companies produce rigid XPS foam with brand names in parentheses: Owens Corning™ (Foamular®) and Dow™ Styrofoam™. Layers of foam can be laminated together using white glue, wood glue, or contact adhesive.

○ **DAP® Alex Plus® Acrylic Latex Caulk:** Alex Plus® Caulk comes in a range of colors, but most often white is the color used in the recipes. This is a caulk made for sealing doors, windows, etc. in homes and is paintable. It is available in smaller squeeze tubes as well as 10-ounce containers requiring a caulk gun.

Figure 2.9: Yaley™ Gel Wax®

Figure 2.10: Yaley™ Crème Wax®

Figure 2.11: Polly Plastics™ Moldable Plastic Pellets

Figure 2.12: Design Master® Glossy Wood Tone Spray

Figure 2.13: Flexible polyurethane foam

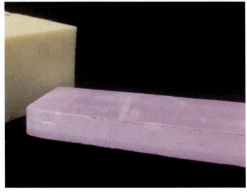

Figure 2.14: Rigid extruded polystyrene (XPS) foam

Figure 2.15: DAP® Alex Plus® Acrylic Latex Caulk

Advanced Tools and Products

- **Cutting and Shaping Tools:**
  - **Band Saw:** A band saw is a stationary power tool with a continuous blade driven around two large wheels. This saw can cut materials up to 6" (or more) thick depending on the model. It can make freeform cuts because it doesn't have a fence.
  - **Dremel® Tool:** This is a brand name for a versatile rotary hand tool that can be used to cut, shape, sand, and buff various materials such as wood, plastic, and foam. There is an assortment of attachments available from engraving tips to sanding to cutting discs.
- **Adhesives and Coatings:**
  - **Contact Adhesive (Nonflammable):** 3M™ Fastbond™ Contact Adhesive 30NF or DAP® Weldwood® Contact Cement are both a water-soluble contact cement that works well for laminating foam in layers. It creates a high-strength bond on contact when both surfaces are dry. It is often referred to as "green glue," even though it comes in green or a neutral color. Gloves are recommended when using this product. Although this product is water based, it is extremely difficult to remove from brushes or rollers. Most artisans will wrap the brush, roller, and roller pan used for contact adhesive in plastic until they are completely finished using the contact adhesive on a project. Then the brush and roller cover are discarded.
  - **Liquid Latex:** Liquid latex is often used for special effects makeup in the entertainment industry. Two different liquid latex products were used in some of the recipes: Castin'Craft® Mold Builder that contains ammonia but is readily available in craft stores like Michael's® and Walmart®, and Kangaroo® Liquid Latex that is ammonia-free and available online at Amazon.com. Liquid latex containing ammonia should only be

Figure 2.16: 3M™ Fastbond™ Contact Adhesive 30NF

Figure 2.17: Liquid latex

used in a well-ventilated area because the fumes can cause irritation. The ammonia-free liquid latex has less odor and tends to cause less irritation. For the recipes, the liquid latex was used to create a texture simulating cooked meat.

- **Rosco® CrystalGel:** Rosco® CrystalGel is an extremely versatile water-based coating that has adhesive properties. It air-dries quickly and has a flexible, translucent surface. It is paintable and tintable. This product is used in over 25% of the recipes in this book. Although it is slightly more expensive, the range of techniques it can achieve far outweighs the additional cost.
- **Rosco® FlexBond:** Rosco® FlexBond is a similar product to Elmer's® Glue-All®, but it creates a stronger and more pliable bond between materials. This product creates a flexible bond between materials such as fabric, woods, and plastics.
- **Rosco® FoamCoat and Rosco® FlexCoat:** Rosco® FoamCoat and Rosco® FlexCoat are both water-based flexible coatings for ethafoam, Styrofoam™, and

Figure 2.20A: Rosco® FoamCoat
Credit: Rosco® Labs

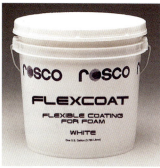

Figure 2.20B: Rosco® FlexCoat
Credit: Rosco® Labs

Figure 2.18: Rosco® CrystalGel
Credit: Rosco® Labs

Figure 2.19: Rosco® FlexBond
Credit: Rosco® Labs

polystyrene foam. When foams have an initial basecoat of one of these products it substantially reduces the chances of the paint flaking off. These coatings adhere to the foam and flex with the foam. The coating also creates a "tooth," a textured surface, to which the paint will stick. Scenic paint, latex house paint, or acrylic paint applied directly to the surface of foam without first applying a flexible coating, such as these, Sculpt or Coat®, or CrystalGel, will dry brittle and flake off when the foam is handled.

- **Sculptural Arts Coating, Inc. Sculpt or Coat®:** Sculpt or Coat® is similar to Rosco® CrystalGel. It coats foam and other materials, creates textures, is an adhesive, and it can be tinted. It is available in a quart and a two-gallon container, which Rosco® CrystalGel is not. At time of printing, the quart is about $30. It is slightly less expensive than Rosco® CrystalGel, too.

- **Paints and Sealers:**
  - **Rosco® Off Broadway™ and Supersaturated™:** Rosco® Off Broadway™ and Supersaturated™ are used repeatedly in many recipes throughout this book. The cost of these paints is more expensive than acrylics from the local art and craft store, but they are worth the cost difference. For less than $100, a kit of 26 one-ounce

samples of every color of Off Broadway™ paint including Clear Flat and Clear Gloss sealers or a kit of 28 one-ounce samples of every Supersaturated™ color available can be purchased. Both product lines are concentrated vinyl acrylic paints that can be diluted with water. The colors mix easily and create rich, vibrant hues.

- **Sculptural Arts Coating, Inc. Artist's Choice Saturated Scenic Paints™:** Artist's Choice Saturated Scenic Paints™ is a concentrated water-based acrylic paint. It is available in a variety of colors that can be used straight out of the can or be diluted with up to 20 parts water depending on the desired effect. A sampler kit is also available for less than $100. It contains 30 one-ounce samples of every Artist's Choice Saturated Scenic Paints™, Sculpt or Coat®, and Plastic Varnish™.
- **Rosco® Clear Acrylic Sealers:** Rosco® Clear Acrylic Sealers come in two finishes: Gloss and Flat, or mix the two together for a Satin. It is a durable finish, but not quite as hard as a urethane finish. It can be added to diluted Rosco® Scenic Paints (or other latex/acrylic paints) to create glazes.
- **Rosco® Premiere Clear Water Based Polyurethane:** Rosco® Premiere Clear is an advanced water-based urethane coating that provides a long-lasting durability,

Figure 2.21A: Rosco® Scenic Paints
Credit: Rosco® Labs

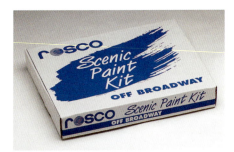

Figure 2.21B: Rosco® Off Broadway™ Scenic Paint Kit
Credit: Rosco® Labs

Figure 2.21C: Sculptural Arts Coating, Inc. family of products
Credit: Sculptural Arts Coating, Inc.

tools and safety **17**

Figure 2.22: Rosco® Premiere Clear Water Based Polyurethane
Credit: Rosco® Labs

Figure 2.23: Encapso® K

hardness, and abrasion resistant coating. It comes in three finishes: Gloss, Flat, and Satin.

○ **Smooth-On® Casting and Molding Products:** One of the benefits of using many of the Smooth-On® products is no gram scale is necessary; it is a simple ratio by volume, and perfect for beginners. The low viscosity of the products offers easy mixing and pouring. All of the Smooth-On® products used in the recipes in this book were created with trial-size kits. Each trial-size kit cost less than $35 including shipping.

○ **Encapso® K:** Encapso® K is a clear encapsulation rubber. It is a two-part liquid mixed together in equal parts. It cures to a soft rubber texture like a high bounce ball. Without any colorant, it is clear as water. It lasts a long time. Projects, like the lemonade, that used Encapso® K have lasted over five years and still look as good as the first day they were made. After it is cured, you can shave the Encapso® K with a knife or crumble it to look like broken glass, diamonds, or ice. You can add color to it with Silc Pig® or Ignite® color pigments from Smooth-On®. This product can be used to create sauces and various drinks.

○ **OOMOO®:** OOMOO® is a mold-making material. It is an easy to use, inexpensive silicone rubber, and cures at room temperature with little shrinkage. The two parts are different colors that make it evident when it is has been stirred thoroughly. It is fairly resistant to tearing when making multiple casts. This product is used in several recipes in this book.

○ **Mold Release:** Smooth-On® has two mold release products, Universal® Mold Release and Mann Ease Release®. Both products come in aerosol and liquid. For the most up-to-date recommendations of which mold release works best with a specific Smooth-On® casting product, consult the Smooth-On® website. Mann Ease Release® 200 is an excellent all-purpose release agent for making molds and casting. It will release polyurethane elastomers, epoxy resins, polyester resins, RTV silicones, rubber, and thermoplastic polymers. It will also work on aluminum, chrome, RTV silicone, epoxy, rubber, and steel molds, according to the Smooth-On® website.

- **Smooth-Cast® 300:** Smooth-Cast® 300 is a casting material. It has a bright white finish that is durable, paintable, and virtually bubble-free. It captures a tremendous amount of detail. It has a curing time of 10 minutes allowing for many casts to be made in quick succession.
- **FlexFoam-iT!®:** FlexFoam-iT!® is a line of flexible polyurethane foams that has a broad selection of formulations of density and expansion. In this book, FlexFoam-iT!® III and V were used in recipes ranging from over-easy eggs to doughnuts to beer. They are castable and expandable foams.
- **Silc Pig®:** Silc Pig® is concentrated silicone color pigment for Smooth-On® silicone products. A little goes a long way and it is possible to mix different Silc Pig® pigments to create custom colors.

Figure 2.24: Smooth-Cast® 300

Figure 2.25: OOMOO®

Figure 2.26: FlexFoam-iT!® III

Figure 2.27: Silc Pig®

Figure 2.28A: Universal® Mold Release

Figure 2.28B: Ease Release®

Safety

Safety is key when making fake food or any of these recipes. Always read and follow the manufacturer's instructions for application, storage, and personal protection. When working with power tools or chemicals, wear safety glasses or chemical goggles. Depending on the material and tools being used, a full-face shield may be a necessary addition to the safety glasses. For most of the products used in this cookbook, safety glasses should be fine but when carving/shaping foam a face shield may be useful. Hearing protection is extremely important when using power tools such as a jig saw, orbital sander, Dremel®, and band saw. Hearing protection comes in a variety of styles—custom molded earplugs, reusable polyurethane memory foam plugs, foam buds on a band or string, or muffs on a headband—to suit your personal preference. Clothing should be appropriate for the job. Long flowing clothing, scarves, and dangly jewelry should not be worn. The chances are good that you will be getting paint or some kind of adhesive or coating on your clothes, and long sleeves, long pants, and closed-toe shoes are recommended. Also, aprons can be helpful to protect your clothing when mixing different casting/mold-making materials. Gloves are important to protect your hands from chemicals, paints, and glues. Disposable latex, vinyl, or nitrile gloves are available depending on your preference and the chemicals being used. Refer to the SDS (Safety Data Sheets) for each product used. SDS sheets are provided by every manufacturer and communicate the hazards, PPEs (personal protection equipment) needed, first aid, and proper handling and storage procedures. On the companion website, we have provided links for SDS sheets for each product used in this book. In the event a product was inadvertently not included, SDS sheets can be found on the manufacturer's website. Be sure to consult a glove chart to determine which glove will most effectively protect your hands. When working with any product, be conscious of the fumes produced. Work in a well-ventilated area with either exhaust fans or a spray hood. A first-aid kit should be readily available as well as an eye-wash station in case of eye contamination. The last chapters devoted to making a few edible food props can be found on the companion website. Always check with all actors and crew for food allergies and sensitivities.

Basic Safety Equipment Checklist

- Eye Protection
- Hearing Protection
- Gloves
- Long Sleeves
- Closed-Toe Shoes
- First-Aid Kit

three
salt dough recipes

Prep Time: 15 minutes

Traditional Salt Dough Recipe

Ingredients

2 c. Flour
1 c. Salt
¾ c. Water

Mix salt and flour together in a large bowl. Gradually stir in water. Mix well until it forms a doughy consistency. Turn dough on to the table and knead with your hands until smooth and combined. Bake at 350°F. The amount of time for baking depends on the size and thickness of the salt dough creations.

The above recipe was found online at: www.learning4kids.net/2012/12/09/how-to-make-salt-dough-recipe/

Version 1

Why This Works—The traditional salt dough recipe has less salt and no vegetable oil or alum. The vegetable oil and alum help to keep the dough from cracking while rolling it into shape.

Ingredients

2 c. Flour
2 c. Salt
1 c. Water
2 tbsp. Vegetable Oil
2 tbsp. Alum

To make the salt dough, mix the dry ingredients together, add water and vegetable oil. Stir thoroughly until there are no more clumps. It should become a doughy consistency. Then knead it until it is smooth and thick. Make a ball. Roll it out to the desired shape and thickness.

Version 2—Heated on Stove

Why This Works—The traditional salt dough recipe has less salt and no vegetable oil or alum. The vegetable oil and alum help to keep the dough from cracking while rolling it into shape. Heating the ingredients on the stove makes the dough less sticky when rolling it out.

Ingredients

2 c. Flour
2 c. Salt
1 c. Water
2 tbsp. Vegetable Oil
2 tbsp. Alum

To make the salt dough, mix the dry ingredients in a saucepan. Add water and vegetable oil. Heat over low heat until it is the consistency of mashed potatoes, stirring until there are no more clumps. Using a plastic spoon, scoop it out on to a lightly floured surface. Knead it until it is smooth and thick. Make a ball. Roll it out to the desired shape and thickness.

Version 3 for Apple Tart

Why This Works—This recipe has one less cup of salt, so the dough remains more flexible and stays soft longer while kneading. Also, this dough was cooked at 200° for an hour rather than 350°F for 20 minutes like the other recipes. The lower temperature keeps the dough from bubbling, but it extends the cooking time. Cooking at lower temperature to keep the dough from bubbling would work on any of the salt dough recipes.

Ingredients

2 c. Flour
1 c. Salt
1 c. Water
2 tbsp. Vegetable Oil
2 tbsp. Alum

To make the salt dough, mix the dry ingredients in a saucepan. Add water and vegetable oil. Heat over low heat until it is the consistency of mashed potatoes, stirring until there are no more clumps. Using a plastic spoon, scoop it out on to a lightly floured surface. Knead it until it is smooth and thick. Make a ball. Roll it out to the desired shape and thickness.

Storing Salt Dough

Unbaked dough can be stored about three days in an airtight container like a plastic food storage bag or container. It can be refrigerated or not. It doesn't seem to make a difference on the longevity.

Baked salt dough will last at least a year when stored properly. First, make sure the item is completely dry, then place in a zippered storage bag, remove all the air from the bag, and seal the bag. Place the bag in a plastic storage bin with a tight-fitting lid.

Section 2

appetizers

four

bread

*baguette, round sourdough bread,
half loaf of a rustic round, and rye loaf*

Baguette Time: 3 hours
Sourdough Time: 3 hours
Half Loaf of a Rustic Round Time: 3 hours
Rye Bread Loaf Time: 1 hour prep, 8 hours to cure

Why This Works—FlexFoam-iT!® III expands 15 times its initial volume. It rises and cures quickly to a solid urethane flexible foam. FlexFoam-iT!® III is the lowest density foam and expands the most. It is important to note that tinted Gel Wax® will bleed into the FlexFoam-iT!® III if the foam isn't sealed. Use Ease Release® 2831 to release the urethane foam from most surfaces.

If you use a Teflon®-coated loaf pan, there is no need to use a mold release agent. If you use Universal® Mold Release alone, it will cause the foam to shrivel according to the Smooth-On® website. For this recipe, the desired effect was to have the top collapse to get a more irregular bread top.

To laminate rigid extruded polystyrene (XPS) foam, wood glue, or contact adhesive can be used successfully. The nonflammable or water-based contact adhesive is preferred because of the ease of clean up and it doesn't "eat" the foam.

Latex house paint was used for these recipes because it was left over from another project in the shop. Any acrylic paint will work.

Safety Precautions

- Always read and follow all manufacturers' directions.
- Always double-check the SDS (Safety Data Sheets) for each product used and make sure the components of the product are not harmful. Companies often change the chemical makeup of their products over the years; don't assume that by checking the SDS once that the product is safe that the product will always be safe to use.
- Wear gloves and safety glasses when working with Smooth-On® products. Use in a well-ventilated area and avoid directly inhaling mixing agents.
- Always wear the appropriate personal protection equipment when working with power tools.

Ingredients

Baguette
4 Pieces of 3½" × 22" × 1" Rigid Extruded Polystyrene (XPS) Foam (commonly known as pink or blue insulation foam)
Titebond® Wood Glue II or Water-Based Contact Adhesive
Rosco® FlexCoat
Acrylic Paint, Tan Valspar® Gentle Shadows 22-1B was used
Bulls Eye® Amber Shellac
Design Master® Glossy Wood Tone Spray

Sourdough Bread
3 Pieces of 10" Diameter × 1" Rigid Extruded Polystyrene (XPS) Foam (commonly known as pink or blue insulation foam)
Titebond® Wood Glue II
Rosco® FlexCoat
Acrylic Paint, Tan Valspar® Gentle Shadows 22-1B was used because it was left over from a previous show
Bulls Eye® Amber Shellac
Design Master® Glossy Wood Tone Spray
Rosco® Premiere Clear Water Based Polyurethane Gloss

Half Loaf of a Rustic Round
2 Pieces of 10" Diameter × 1" Rigid Extruded Polystyrene (XPS) Foam (commonly known as pink or blue insulation foam)
3M™ Fastbond™ Contact Adhesive 30NF or DAP® Weldwood® Contact Cement
Acrylic Paint, Tan Valspar® Gentle Shadows 22-1B was used because it was left over from a previous show
Acrylic Paint, Warm Light Brown Sherwin-Williams® Hopsack SW6109, left over from a previous show
Sawdust
Design Master® Glossy Wood Tone Spray
Bulls Eye® Amber Shellac

> **Rye Loaf**
> Smooth-On® FlexFoam-iT!® III
> Smooth-On® Ease Release® 2831 (or Ease Release® 200) Mold Release Aerosol Spray
> Smooth-On® Silc Pig® Brown Concentrated Pigment for Silicone
> Sawdust
> Design Master® Glossy Wood Tone Spray
> Bulls Eye® Amber Shellac

Tools

- C-Clamps or Quick Grip® Bar Clamps
- Japanese Ryoba Saw
- Band Saw
- Stanley® Surform® Shaver™ or Pocket Plane™ or Sandpaper
- Orbital Sander or Sandpaper, optional
- Bread Loaf Pan
- 3 Clear Plastic 8 oz. cups
- Paint brushes
- Sea Sponge
- Gloves
- Stirring Stick

Baguette

Cut 3 pieces of 1" rigid extruded polystyrene foam 3½" × 22". Apply a uniform coat of Titebond® Premium Wood Glue II to each piece of foam. Stack one layer on top of the next. Make sure the glue is touching the entire surface of each layer. Clamp or place a heavy object on the stack of the three layers of foam to prevent sliding and air pockets between layers while the glue is drying. Allow the glue to cure for at least 1 hour before trying to shape the foam. The glue fully cures in 8 hours.

Shape the edges using a Stanley® Surform® Shaver™. The edges should be rounded and tapered. There should be

Figure 4.1: Shaped baguette and half of a rustic round bread

diagonal slashes about every 2" based on research images; carve and shape these slashes so they look like they were made in the dough before it was baked and then puffed up in the baking process. Once the general shape is created, an orbital or palm sander can be used to smooth out the overall shape of the foam, if a smoother surface is desired.

Apply a coat of Rosco® FlexCoat to prevent the paint from flaking off the foam when the baguette is handled. Let dry.

Apply a basecoat of Valspar® Gentle Shadows 22-1B or similar acrylic paint color; mixing Rosco® Off Broadway™ White and Raw or Earth Umber would yield a similar result. Allow to dry completely. Apply an even light coat of Bulls Eye® Amber Shellac to the entire surface of the bread and let dry.

In a well-ventilated area or under a spray hood, the baguette can be toned by spraying Design Master® Glossy Wood Tone on areas that might have browned more in the cooking process.

28 appetizers

Figure 4.2: Rough shape of sourdough bread

Sourdough Bread

Cut 3 pieces of 1" rigid extruded polystyrene foam 10" in diameter. Use Titebond® Premium Wood Glue II to laminate the layers of foam by applying a uniform coat to each piece. Stack one layer on top of another layer to create a piece of foam that is 10" diameter and 3" thick. Make sure the glue is touching the entire surface of each layer. Clamp or place a heavy object on the stack of foam to prevent sliding and air pockets between layers while the glue is drying. Allow the glue to cure for at least 1 hour before carving.

Shape the edges using a Stanley® Surform® Shaver™ to approximate the form of a loaf of sourdough bread found in your research image. Create a valley in the center of the top so it looks like it has been scored before baking and then risen during the baking process to create a "bread ear." A bread ear is the scored opening on a loaf of bread. Sand to smooth out texture, if desired.

Apply a coat of Rosco® FlexCoat to prevent the paint from flaking off the foam when the bread is handled. Let dry. *Note: If Rosco® FoamCoat was used instead of Rosco® FlexCoat, then the loaf could be sanded* after *the FoamCoat has dried.*

Apply a basecoat of Valspar® Gentle Shadows 22-1B or similar acrylic paint color; mixing Rosco® Off Broadway™ White and Raw or Earth Umber would yield a similar result. Allow to dry completely. Apply an even light coat of Bulls Eye® Amber Shellac to the entire surface of the bread.

After the shellac has dried, the bread can be toned by spraying Design Master® Glossy Wood Tone on areas that might have browned more in the cooking process. Apply a light coat of Rosco® Premiere Clear Water Based Polyurethane Gloss.

Figure 4.3: Toning sourdough bread with Design Master® Glossy Wood Tone Spray

Half Loaf of a Rustic Round

Cut 2 pieces of 1" rigid extruded polystyrene foam 10" in diameter. Cut the circles in half, so you have 4 half-circles of 1" XPS foam. Use a water-based contact adhesive to laminate the layers of foam by applying a uniform coat to each piece. Both surfaces that are to be glued together need to be coated with contact adhesive. Allow the contact adhesive to dry completely, about 30 minutes. Stack one layer on top of another layer to create a piece of foam that is a 10" diameter semicircle and 4" thick. Make sure the glue is touching the entire surface of each layer. Clamp or place a heavy object on the stack of foam to prevent air pockets between layers while the glue is drying. Allow the glue to cure for at least 1 hour before carving.

Round and shape the edges using a Stanley® Surform® Shaver™ to reflect the research image. Create an undulating surface on the top of the bread that is characteristic of a round rustic loaf. This should look like someone has sliced a round loaf of bread in half.

Apply a coat of Rosco® FlexCoat to prevent the paint from flaking off the foam when the bread is handled. Let dry.

Apply a basecoat of Valspar® Gentle Shadows 22-1B or similar acrylic paint color; mixing Rosco® Off Broadway™ White and Raw or Earth Umber would yield a similar result. Sprinkle sawdust all over the outside crust while the paint is still wet. Let dry completely. Lightly sponge or stipple Sherwin-Williams® Hopsack SW6109 or similar acrylic paint; mixing Rosco® Off Broadway™ White, Raw Sienna, and Burnt Umber or Burnt Sienna would yield a similar result. Don't sponge too much of this darker brown, because it will flatten out the texture by creating a visually muddy surface. Allow to dry completely.

In a well-ventilated area or under a spray hood, the bread can be toned by spraying Design Master® Glossy Wood Tone on areas that might have browned more in the cooking process. Apply Bulls Eye® Amber Shellac sparingly to certain areas on the surface of the bread.

Figure 4.4: Mixing Smooth-On® FlexFoam-iT!® III for rye bread

Rye Loaf

The rye loaf of bread is made by using Smooth-On® FlexFoam-iT!® III. It is a two-part urethane foam. The parts are determined by volume. Measure 1 part Part A and 2 parts Part B into separate plastic containers. *Tip: use three identical plastic cups to measure and mark the same portion (1 part) in each cup—one container for A, one for B, and a second container for B.* The website suggests pre-mixing Part B with a mechanical mixer or drill before adding Part A *into* Part B. Add a small amount of Silc Pig® Brown Concentrated Pigment to the mixture of A and B. Mix vigorously for 30 seconds before pouring. Make sure you stir thoroughly and scrape the sides and bottom of the cup. You need to work quickly because you will only have about 5 more seconds to pour it. The pot life is about 35 seconds. Pour into the bread pan. The foam will be tacky to the touch after 30 minutes and it will be completely set in 2 hours.

Figure 4.5: Pouring Smooth-On® FlexFoam-iT!® III with Silc Pig® brown pigment into loaf pan

Figure 4.6: Smooth-On® FlexFoam-iT!® III with Silc Pig® brown pigment in loaf pan

Cover the loaf pan with wax paper after pouring the FlexFoam-iT!® III into the pan. The wax paper will prevent the foam from becoming a smooth solid crust while it cures; leaving a pock-marked surface.

Remove from pan. Apply an even coat of Bulls Eye® Amber Shellac to cover the bread. Sprinkle top with sawdust. Apply another even coat of Bulls Eye® Amber Shellac to cover the bread and adhere all the sawdust. In a well-ventilated area or under a spray hood, the bread can be toned by spraying Design Master® Glossy Wood Tone on areas that might have browned more in the cooking process. Leave some areas untouched by Glossy Wood Tone Spray and some areas can have a heavier coat. Let dry completely before handling.

Figure 4.7: Smooth-On® FlexFoam-iT!® III out of the loaf pan

bread   **31**

Figure 4.8: Sawdust sprinkled on top of Smooth-On® FlexFoam-iT!® III

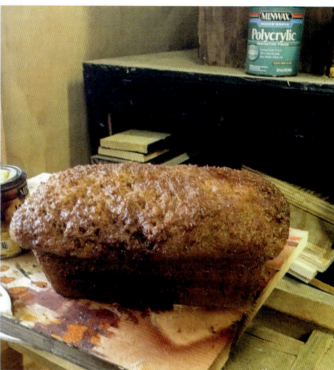

Figure 4.9: Toned rye bread

five

cheese platter

Brie, Cheddar, Swiss, and Gouda

Total Prep Time: 10 hours
Total Dry Time: 24 hours

Why This Works—Fake cheese is expensive and may not come in the form needed for the show. The gel candle wax has a realistic weight for the end product. It is tintable and durable. When crème wax is added to the gel wax, it gives the gel wax more structure and reduces the bubbles and the wax will set faster. Adding more crème wax to the gel wax allows the gel wax to set faster, but it can be harder to cut once it has hardened. For a softer cheese, use a 2:1 ratio of gel wax to crème wax. Both are low-density candle waxes that are long lasting and odorless.

Adding a dash of color from the Yaley™ concentrated candle dye to the wax tints the entire wax. All of Yaley's candle dyes are compatible with the gel wax. If the budget is an issue, there has been success in tinting the wax by using crayons.

Show Application—This cheese tray was built for University of Cincinnati College-Conservatory of Music's production of the opera *Don Giovanni*. It was used in the banquet scene in Act I. The actors pretended to eat from it.

Safety Precautions

- Don't pour any wax down the drain.
- Never leave melting wax unattended.
- Use a thermometer to monitor the temperature of the wax.
  - Don't overheat the wax. It will melt around 130°F. The optimum temperature is between 160°F and 170°F. Heat to a maximum of 220°F.
- Keep the wax away from an open flame.
- Always use a potholder when handling a hot pot.
- Always keep an ABC fire extinguisher nearby.
- Some liquid latex contains ammonia. Be sure to use in a well-ventilated area, avoid eye contact, and read all safety precautions on the label.

Ingredients

Brie
4" block Yaley™ Gel Wax®
2" block Yaley™ Crème Wax®
Yaley™ Yellow Concentrated Candle Dye
DAP® Alex Plus® Caulk

Cheddar Cheese
3" block Yaley™ Gel Wax®
3" block Yaley™ Crème Wax®
Yaley™ Yellow Concentrated Candle Dye
Yaley™ Red Concentrated Candle Dye

Swiss Cheese
4" block Yaley™ Gel Wax®
2" block Yaley™ Crème Wax®
Yaley™ Yellow Concentrated Candle Dye
Yaley™ White Concentrated Candle Dye

Gouda
3" block Yaley™ Gel Wax®
3" block Yaley™ Crème Wax®
Yaley™ Yellow Concentrated Candle Dye
Yaley™ Red Concentrated Candle Dye
Design Master® Glossy Wood Tone Spray

Tools

- Smooth-On® Universal® Mold Release Aerosol Spray
- Candle Thermometer
- Ceramic Mold (a shallow round baking dish)
- 8" or 9" Round Cake Pan
- Hot Knife
- Saucepan

Brie Cheese—Total Time: 4 Hours

Melt a 4" block of Gel Wax® and a 2" block of Crème Wax® in a saucepan on low heat. Add small shavings of yellow candle dye until you reach the desired color. Spray the ceramic dish, the mold, with Universal® Mold Release. Pour molten wax into the ceramic dish.

Once the wax has set, remove it from the mold and place it on a clean surface. Coat the wheel with DAP® Alex Plus® Caulk (white). It works best to smooth the caulk with your wet fingers with water. *Wear gloves*.

Let caulk cure overnight or until it has hardened completely.

Figure 5.1: Melting wax for cheese

Figure 5.3: Cheese wheel covered in Alex Plus® Caulk

Figure 5.2: Unmolded wax

Figure 5.4: Cutting brie with hot knife on wax paper

Figure 5.5: Completed brie cheese wheel with a piece removed

Figure 5.6: Cheddar cheese wheel

Place the cheese on wax paper. Use a hot knife to cut the cheese wheel into wedges. The hot knife will melt the wax and make the sides of each piece smooth. The wax paper will protect the work surface from the dripping and puddling of the wax.

Cheddar Cheese—Total Time: 2 Hours

Melt equal parts of both Gel Wax® and Crème Wax® in a saucepan on low heat. Add yellow and red concentrated dye to reach the desired color of cheddar cheese. Spray the ceramic dish, the mold, with Universal® Mold Release. Check wax temperature with candle thermometer prior to pouring. Pour molten wax into a round, ceramic baking dish of a similar size as the research. Once the wax is cool, remove it from the mold, and cut it into wedges (or whatever shape you desire) with a hot knife. *Place the cheese on wax paper when using a hot knife. The hot knife melts the wax as you cut it. The wax will drip and puddle around the cheese. Remove the cheese pieces before the wax sets.*

Figure 5.7: Swiss cheese wedges

Swiss Cheese—Total Time: 2 Hours
Melt 2 parts Gel Wax® and 1 part Crème Wax® in a saucepan on low heat. Once the wax is completely melted, add white and yellow candle dye colorant shavings to tint to the desired color of Swiss cheese. Spray the round metal cake pan, the mold, with Universal® Mold Release. Pour into the metal cake pan. Wax will set in about 2 hours. Remove from the mold and cut into wedges (or whatever shape you desire) with a regular knife because the wax is softer than that created for the brie. Use a ³⁄₈" twist drill bit to make the holes. For additional realism, use different size drill bits to have a variety of holes. The wax doesn't crumble or break when drilling holes.

Figure 5.8: Holes drilled into wax for Swiss cheese

Figure 5.9: Wax coated with liquid latex to create a Gouda cheese wheel

Gouda Cheese—Total Time: 2 Hours
Using equal parts of both Gel Wax® and Crème Wax® melt the wax in a saucepan on low heat. Add yellow and red concentrated dye to reach the desired color of Gouda cheese from the research. Spray the ceramic baking dish mold with Universal® Mold Release. Pour molten wax into the ceramic baking dish. Once the wax is cooled, remove it from the mold. In a well-ventilated area, coat wheel with liquid latex to replicate the rind of Gouda cheese. In a well-ventilated area or under a spray hood, use Design Master® Glossy Wood Tone Spray Paint to tone the rind of the cheese wheel. You can cut it into wedges (or whatever shape you desire) with a hot knife. *Place the cheese on wax paper when using a hot knife. The wax will drip and puddle as you cut it.*

Figure 5.10: Completed cheese wedges ready for arrangement on serving tray

six

chicken wings

38   appetizers

Total Prep Time: 15 minutes per wing casting, 90 minutes painting with clear coat
Total Dry Time: 6 hours for mold to cure
Total Time: 8 hours

Why This Works—The benefit of some Smooth-On® products is that no scale is necessary for weighing the components. It is a simple 1:1 ratio by volume, which is perfect for beginners. The low viscosity of the products offers easy mixing and pouring. Smooth-Cast® 300 has a bright white finish that is durable, paintable, and virtually bubble free and it captures a tremendous amount of detail. One trial-size kit of Smooth-Cast® 300 could yield 12–15 wings.

OOMOO® 30 is easy to use, an inexpensive silicone rubber molding material, and cures at room temperature with little shrinkage. The two parts are different colors (Part A is pink, Part B is blue) that make it evident when it is has been stirred thoroughly. It is fairly resistant to tearing after de-molding a series of casts.

According to the experts at Smooth-On®, when creating a mold from a model that is porous or organic, the model needs to be sealed with an acrylic spray like Krylon® Crystal Clear Acrylic to prevent failure in the mold process. After it has dried, Mann Ease Release® 200 needs to be applied. Ease Release® 200 is an excellent all-purpose release agent for making molds and casting.

Safety Precautions

- Always wear gloves and safety glasses when working with Smooth-On® products.
- Use in a well-ventilated area and avoid directly inhaling mixing agents.
- Read and follow all manufacturers' instructions.

Show Application—This method could be used to create fried chicken required in *Assassins*. There is a blog with information on how to create fried chicken: http://fake-n-bake.blogspot.com/2012_10_01_archive.html. In the blog, a plaster mold is used. The flexibility of a silicone rubber mold is favorable in the casting process. Plaster can break if dropped; OOMOO® captures great detail and doesn't rip or tear easily.

Ingredients

Actual Chicken Wings for Casting
Krylon® Crystal Clear Acrylic Spray
Smooth-On® OOMOO® 30
Mann Ease Release® 200
Smooth-On® Smooth-Cast® 300
Bulls Eye® Amber Shellac
Rosco® Off Broadway™ Scenic Paint: Fire Red, Burnt Sienna, Orange, Deep Red
Rosco® Premiere Clear Water Based Polyurethane Gloss or Rosco® Clear Acrylic Gloss

Tools

- 3/16" Foam-core board to create a box
- Utility Knife
- Cutting Mat
- Clear Plastic 8 oz. cups
- Larger Mixing Container, optional (a larger cup leaves room to stir)
- Small Artist Paint Brushes
- Hot Glue Gun
- Clorox® Disinfecting Wipes
- Nitrile Gloves
- Safety Glasses

Create a mold box by cutting foam-core board in pieces to create a box. The box should be 1" to 2" larger than the chicken wings you are casting. Hot glue the pieces of foam-core board together as an open-top box. If the wings have sauce on them,

chicken wings   **39**

Figure 6.1: Chicken wings in box to be cast

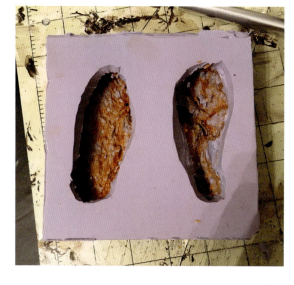

Figure 6.2: Mold for wings with wing sauce residue on mold

wash off all sauce so it doesn't come off in the mold. Coat the chicken wings with shellac or Krylon® Crystal Clear Acrylic Spray. Once the wings are completely dry, hot glue chicken wings to the bottom of mold box. It is important to glue the object firmly in place before making the mold. Liberally spray the wings and the foam-core board with Ease Release® 200. Let it dry for at least 5 minutes before pouring the mold as the instructions recommend.

The silicone rubber of OOMOO® 30 will create a negative mold of the wings. Fill half of an 8 oz. plastic cup with Part A. Pour 4 oz. of Part B into the cup with Part A, which should fill the cup. You will have 8 oz. of product that will need to be combined. Using a larger graduated mixing container that is larger than 8 oz. will give you room to mix the two parts. Stir until the pink and blue liquids turn purple. You will only have 30 minutes to work with this mixture. Pour the OOMOO® 30 into the mold box at the lowest point and cover the chicken wings completely including at least ½" above the highest point on the wings. Allow the OOMOO® 30 to set for 6 hours.

To remove the mold from the mold box, cut along the hot-glued corners. Carefully, remove the wings from the mold. You will need to make relief cuts in the OOMOO® around the wings to remove them because of their shape. Relief cuts create more flexibility in the mold to remove the wings since they don't have a flat side. Make sure you tape the OOMOO® mold back together before casting wings. Medical tape worked, but masking tape and Scotch™ tape did not. If there is Buffalo sauce residue in the mold, wipe the mold clean with a Clorox® Disinfecting Wipe. Smooth-Cast® 300 will be used to create the positive chicken wings. Let the mold dry, then spray it with Ease Release® 200.

Smooth-Cast® 300 uses equal parts of Part A and Part B. Pour ½" of Part A into a plastic cup, followed by ½" of Part B into a separate cup so you can accurately assess that you have equal parts. Combine into a single cup and stir thoroughly. The mixture has a pot life of 3 minutes. Pour the clear liquid into the mold. The liquid will turn white as it cures. The wings will be ready to be removed from the mold in 15 minutes. The mold will become hot because Smooth-Cast® 300 generates heat as it cures.

Figure 6.4: Casting chicken wings with Smooth-On® 300 soon after pouring

Figure 6.3: Part A and Part B measured out in plastic cups

Figure 6.5: Casting chicken wings with Smooth-On® 300 ready to be removed

chicken wings 41

Paint the wings to match research. For this project, Rosco® Off Broadway™ colors of Fire Red, Burnt Sienna, Orange, and Deep Red were used. Let dry.

Coat the wings with a coat of Rosco® Premiere Clear Water Based Polyurethane Gloss.

Figure 6.6: Cast chicken wings

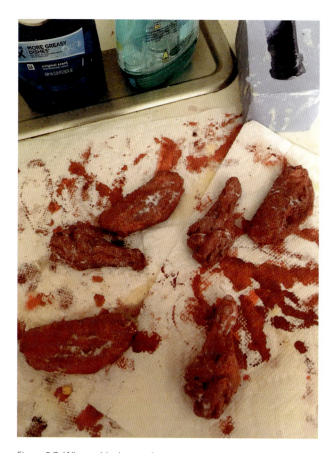

Figure 6.7: Wings with clear sealer

seven

egg rolls, spring rolls, and soy sauce

egg rolls, spring rolls, and soy sauce

Total Prep Time: 1 hour 30 minutes
Total Dry Time: 24 hours

Why This Works—The traditional salt dough recipe has less salt and no vegetable oil or alum. The vegetable oil and alum help to keep the dough from cracking while rolling it into shape. Heating the ingredients on the stove makes the dough less sticky when rolling it out. The vegetable oil and extra salt have an added benefit of giving a pockmarked texture that resembles the fried texture of an egg roll and a spring roll. Thai Unryu paper is a lightweight and translucent paper. It has long winding kozo fibers that run organically throughout the paper. When it is torn, it creates a soft feathered edge. For this project, the orange and green paper will simulate the vegetables and shrimp inside the spring rolls. Thai Unryu paper can be found at an art supply store or online. Creative Paperclay® is a modeling material that air-dries. It can easily be sculpted, molded, and shaped while it is moist. It is premixed, so it is a quick way of creating the filling for the rolls. It also has the ability to capture fine details or be sanded, neither of which is needed for this project.

Egg Rolls

Ingredients

Salt Dough
- 2 c. Flour
- 2 c. Salt
- 1 c. Water
- 2 tbsp. Vegetable Oil
- 2 tbsp. Alum

Creative Paperclay®
Bull's Eye® Amber Shellac

Tools

- Rolling Pin
- Saucepan
- Spoon
- Chip Brush
- Nitrile Gloves
- Zippered Plastic Storage Bag

To make the salt dough, mix the dry ingredients in a saucepan. Add water and vegetable oil. Heat over low heat until it is the consistency of mashed potatoes, stirring until there are no more clumps. Using a plastic spoon, scoop it out on to a lightly floured surface (smooth and non-porous). Knead it until it is smooth and thick. Make a ball.

Using a rolling pin, roll dough out so it is less than ⅛" thick. Cut the dough into a square that is 4½" × 4½".

Position the dough with one corner pointed toward you. Referring to your research, add a column of Creative Paperclay®

Figure 7.1: Salt dough rolled and cut into a 4½" × 4½" square

44   appetizers

to the center for the filling. Fold the corner pointing toward you to the center, fold the left and right corners to the center over the Paperclay®, and continue to roll away from you until all of the Paperclay® is completely encapsulated.

Paint the rolled salt dough with amber shellac to achieve the color of fried egg rolls.

Place rolls in a plastic zippered storage bag for 24 hours to dry. The shellac will react to the moisture and salt in the salt dough to create the granular texture of a fried egg roll.

Figure 7.2: Paperclay® wrapped with salt dough

Figure 7.4: After 24 hours of drying in a plastic storage bag

Spring Rolls

Ingredients

Thai Unryu Paper: Green, Orange, and White
Creative Paperclay®
Bull's Eye® Clear Shellac

Figure 7.3: Wrapped dough coated with amber shellac

Tools

- X-Acto Knife or Utility Knife
- Cutting Matt
- Scissors

Start by cutting 4½" × 4½" squares of white Thai Unryu paper for the spring roll wrappers. Cut ⅛" strips of the green and orange Thai Unryu paper then slice them into smaller pieces to represent the vegetables in a spring roll.

Figure 7.6: Rolled spring rolls. Top spring roll is coated with clear shellac

Figure 7.5: Thai Unryu paper cut and prepped to begin making spring rolls

Using the same technique as explained to make the egg rolls, take one white square of Thai Unryu paper, place one corner pointed toward you, and a small amount of tube-shaped Paperclay® and the pieces of green and orange paper to the center. Fold and roll in the same manner as the egg rolls. Finish spring roll by applying a thin layer of clear shellac over entire surface. Let dry according to the directions on the shellac.

Soy Sauce

Ingredients

Yaley™ Gel Wax®
Yaley™ Brown Colorant Block

Tools

- Candle Thermometer
- Saucepan
- Spoon
- Soy Sauce Bowl or Bottle

46   appetizers

Melt Yaley™ Gel Wax® in a saucepan on low and add half a block of brown colorant. (An inexpensive alternative for colorant is to use an unwrapped crayon.) Stir while melting to combine the gel wax and colorant. Once the gel wax is melted and has an even coloring, pour into the bowl or bottle for the soy sauce and let cool. *Remember that this saucepan and any utensils should never be used to make edible food ever again.*

Figure 7.7: Melted Yaley™ Gel Wax® and brown colorant in saucepan

eight

oysters on the
half shell

48 appetizers

Total Prep Time: 2 hours
Total Dry Time: Overnight, roughly 6 hours

Why This Works—Adding liquid latex to Sculpt or Coat® makes the Sculpt or Coat® opaque and provides the same consistency as actual oyster meat. Artist's Choice™ products were used for this recipe, but Rosco® scenic products (scenic paint and CrystalGel or any acrylic paint) could work. Using a glue syringe for piping aids in creating a consistent bead. Although it is possible to use a small zippered plastic bag with the tip of one corner cut off, this delivery system often takes considerable time to perfect a consistent bead.

Show Application—These oysters were built for University of Cincinnati College-Conservatory of Music's production of the opera *Don Giovanni*. It was used in the banquet scene. The actors pretended to eat them.

Safety Precautions

- Sculptural Arts Coating, Inc. Artist's Choice™ recommends wearing impermeable gloves when using their products, especially for those who are hypersensitive.
- Always wash hands and face before a break and at the end of the workday.
- Cleaned oyster shells can be purchased online or at a craft store. If you buy oysters and shuck them for the shells, use extreme caution.
  - You will want to use an oyster knife or short, thin-edged instrument, even a flat-head screwdriver or table knife to open the oyster shells.
  - Use an oven mitt, gloves, or a towel to hold the oyster shell flat on the table. The shells can be sharp.
  - Hold the oyster with the flatter side up and cupped side down.
  - Look for the hinge and work the knife between the shells to pry them open by twisting the knife blade.
  - Then slide the knife between the shells along the entire length.
  - For a more detailed explanation of how to shuck an oyster see www.wikihow.com/Shuck-Oysters or a how-to video www.youtube.com/watch?v=Uy-rbEXFwLw. Of course, if you are shucking the oysters, all the oyster meat needs to be discarded and the shells need to be cleaned and dried thoroughly.

Ingredients

Oyster Shells
Liquid Latex
Sculptural Arts Coating, Inc. Sculpt or Coat®
Sculptural Arts Coating, Inc. Artist's Choice Saturated Scenic Paints™
  Neutral Tone Gray
  Masking Black
Acrylic Gloss Medium

Tools

- Glue Syringe for piping
- Teaspoon

Figure 8.1: Cleaned oyster shell

Remove any debris from the shell. Make a mixture of 2 parts liquid latex and 1 part Sculpt or Coat® and add Neutral Tone Gray paint to match research image. Let dry.

Figure 8.2: Oyster shells filled with Sculpt or Coat® and latex mixture

Referring to your research images, mix acrylic gloss medium with Neutral Tone gray and Masking Black to create a representation of the oyster's adductor muscle (it's the light gray part). Using a teaspoon, drop a small dollop of the tinted acrylic gloss medium on top of the latex–Sculpt or Coat®. To create the mantel edge (the black edge around the meat of the oyster), combine Sculpt or Coat® and Masking Black paint, then pipe it on the shell using a glue syringe. The oyster will need overnight to cure depending on humidity conditions.

Figure 8.3: Close-up of one completed oyster

Figure 8.4: Close-up of completed oysters

nine

popcorn

Total Prep Time: 30 minutes

Why This Works—While actual popcorn is inexpensive as well as fast and easy to make, one reason to create fake popcorn is that it won't attract unwanted critters to feast on it.

White Polystyrene Industrial Loose Fill S-Shaped packing peanuts are inexpensive. By breaking them up into roughly ¼" lengths, it resembles popcorn and is economical. To make inedible cashews, the same method could be used if the packing peanuts were broken into crescent shapes.

Rosco® FlexBond was used both to coat and to adhere the packing peanuts to the block in the popcorn container. Elmer's® Glue-All® could also be used. The benefit is Elmer's® Glue-All® is slightly less expensive and readily available.

Show Application—*The Rocky Horror Show* by Richard O'Brien or *If You Take a Mouse to the Movies* based on the book by Laura Numeroff and Felicia Bond might use this recipe. For the latter show, the scale might need to be adjusted to match the style of the show.

Safety Precautions

- The packing peanuts can generate a lot of static electricity. You may experience a little static shock when you touch another object after handling the peanuts.
- Always read and follow the manufacturer's directions.

Ingredients

White Polystyrene Industrial Loose Fill S-Shaped Packing Peanuts
3½" × 3½" × 1" Rigid Extruded Polystyrene (XPS) Foam (commonly known as pink or blue insulation foam)
Rosco® FlexBond
Acrylic Paint, Neutral Beige (for this project Valspar® Bubbly V0901, left over from a previous project in the shop was used)
Rosco® Clear Acrylic Gloss™
Dr. Ph. Martin's® Bombay™ India Ink, Yellow

Tools

- Popcorn Container
- X-acto® Knife
- Disposable Gloves—latex, nitrile, or vinyl
- Paint Brushes
- Small Containers for Mixing Paint

Figure 9.1: Foam spacer glued into popcorn container

Cut a piece of XPS foam into a 3½" × 3½" square or slightly smaller than the popcorn container, so the entire bucket doesn't have to be filled with popcorn. Wedge the foam square into the container. Glue in place if desired, or if it isn't a tight fit inside the container.

52   appetizers

Figure 9.2: Polystyrene packing peanuts

Break the 1½" long white polystyrene packing peanuts into smaller pieces of about ¼" in length.

Figure 9.3: Packing peanuts torn into popcorn kernel shapes

Place the kernels on top of the foam block inside the container. Pile them to be seen above the edge of the bucket.

Pour a layer of Rosco® FlexBond on top of the kernels. Let it dry. This will do double duty of securing the kernels and priming them for paint. Before moving the container, let the Rosco® FlexBond begin to set because the kernels tend to move easily.

Figure 9.4: Dr. Ph. Martin's® Bombay™ Yellow India Ink and Rosco® Clear Acrylic Gloss mixed together for butter

Paint the kernels a neutral beige color. For this project, Valspar® Bubbly V0901 was used because it was left over from a previous project in the shop. After that dries, while wearing gloves, mix Dr. Ph. Martin's® Bombay™ Yellow India Ink into a small amount of Rosco® Clear Acrylic Gloss. Pour over the popcorn kernels. Use your finger to spread the ink over the packing peanuts. Gloves will protect your fingers from becoming stained with ink. Let dry.

popcorn 53

Figure 9.5: Completed popcorn

ten

shrimp cocktail

Total Prep Time: 8 hours; a mold of one shrimp takes 15 minutes
Total Dry Time: 24 hours

Why This Works—The benefit for using Smooth-On® products is no scale is necessary for measuring. It is a simple 1:1 ratio by volume, which is perfect for beginners. The low viscosity of the products offers easy mixing and pouring. Smooth-Cast® 300 has a bright white finish that is durable, paintable, and virtually bubble-free. It captures a tremendous amount of detail.

OOMOO® 25 is an inexpensive silicone rubber, easy to use, and cures at room temperature with little shrinkage. The two parts are different colors (Part A is pink, Part B is blue) that make it evident when it is has been stirred thoroughly. It is fairly resistant to tearing after de-molding through a series of casts.

According to the experts at Smooth-On®, when creating a mold from a model that is porous or organic, the model needs to be sealed with an acrylic spray like Krylon® Crystal Clear Acrylic to prevent failure in the mold process. After it has dried, Mann Ease Release® 200 needs to be applied. Ease Release® 200 is an excellent general-purpose release agent and should be used with silicone molds like OOMOO®.

The gel candle wax is tintable, durable, and has a realistic weight for the end product. It is a low-density candle wax that is long lasting and odorless. Adding a dash of color from the Yaley™ concentrated candle dye to the wax tints the entire wax. All of Yaley's candle dyes are compatible with the gel wax. If the budget is an issue, there has been success in tinting the wax by using crayons.

Safety Precautions

- Wear gloves and safety glasses when working with Smooth-On® products. Use in a well-ventilated area and avoid directly inhaling mixing agents.
- Read and follow all manufacturers' instructions.
- Don't pour any wax down the drain.
- Never leave melting wax unattended.
- Use a thermometer to monitor the temperature of the wax.
  - Don't overheat the wax. It will melt around 130°F. The optimum temperature is between 160°F and 170°F. Heat to a maximum of 220°F.
- Keep the wax away from an open flame.
- Always use a potholder when handling a hot pot.
- Always keep an ABC fire extinguisher nearby.

Shrimp

Ingredients

Real Frozen Shrimp for casting
Krylon® Crystal Clear Acrylic Spray
Smooth-On® OOMOO® 25
Smooth-On® Smooth-Cast® 300
Mann Ease Release® 200 Mold Release

Tools

- Foam-core board to create a box
- Utility Knife
- Cutting Mat
- Clear Plastic 8 oz. cup (or a larger cup to leave room to stir liquid)
- Dixie® 3 oz. cup
- Acrylic Paints
- Small Artist Paint Brushes
- Hot Glue Gun
- Glossy Clear Tape
- Clear nail polish

56 appetizers

Figure 10.1: Real shrimp glued in mold box made out of foam-core board

Figure 10.2: Casting Shrimp in a negative mold

Create a mold box by cutting foam-core board into 3 pieces approximately 3" × 6" for the bottom and two sides and 2 pieces approximately 6" × 6" for the ends. Hot glue the pieces together as an open-top box. The box should be 1" to 2" larger than the shrimp. Hot glue a frozen shrimp to the bottom of mold box. The shrimp need to be sealed with an acrylic spray like Krylon® Crystal Clear Acrylic to prevent failure in the mold process. It is important to glue the object firmly in place before making the mold. Spray shrimp and box liberally with Mann Ease Release® 200. The silicone rubber of OOMOO® 25 will create a negative mold of the shrimp. Fill half of an 8 oz. plastic cup with Part A. Pour 4 oz. of Part B into the cup with Part A, which should fill the cup. You will have 8 oz. of product that will need to be combined. Using a larger graduated mixing container that is larger than 8 oz. will give you room to mix the two parts. Stir until the pink and blue liquids turn purple. You will only have 15 minutes to work with this. Pour the OOMOO® 25 into the mold box at the lowest point and cover the shrimp completely. Allow the OOMOO® 25 to set for 75 minutes.

To remove the mold from the mold box, cut along the hot-glued corners. Carefully, remove the shrimp from the mold. You will need to make a cut in the OOMOO® on the side to remove the shrimp because it is a crescent shape. Make sure you tape the mold back together before casting shrimp. Medical tape worked, but masking tape and Scotch™ tape did not. Smooth-On® 300 will be used to create the positive shrimp. It uses equal parts of Part A and Part B. Using a 3 oz. Dixie® cup, pour Part A into the cup about halfway, followed by an equal amount of Part B. Stir thoroughly. Pour the clear liquid into the mold. The liquid will turn white as it cures. The shrimp will be ready to be removed from the mold in 15 minutes.

shrimp cocktail

Figure 10.3: Cast shrimp near mold

Cocktail Sauce

Ingredients

Yaley® Gel Wax®
Yaley™ Red Concentrated Candle Dye
Wood Shavings

Tools

- Saucepan
- Spoon

Figure 10.4: Detail of painted shrimp

Figure 10.5: Detail of cocktail sauce

Using acrylic paint, paint the shrimp to match research image of shrimp. Add definition to the tails of the shrimp by intensifying the color at the tips. Applying a coat of clear nail polish to the tails makes them appear shiny, but doesn't replicate the translucent shell that encases the tip of the tail. Attach glossy Scotch® invisible tape to the end of each tail to simulate the translucent shell.

Making the Cocktail Sauce

Melt a small 2″ × 2″ cube of Yaley® Gel Wax® in a saucepan on low heat. Add a small amount of red concentrated candle dye. Stir. Add small wood shavings to the liquid wax to give the impression of horseradish. Carefully, pour into martini glass. Glue shrimp to rim of the glass.

58 appetizers

Figure 10.6: Finished shrimp and cocktail sauce

eleven

vegetable tray

60   appetizers

Total Prep Time: 1–2 hours
Total Dry Time: 1–3 hours
Total Painting Time: 1–2 hours
Total Time: 4–8 hours

Why This Works—Using Q-tips® Cotton Swabs to paint the Crayola® Model Magic® won't leave brush strokes. A metal ruler has a sharper edge which creates a good crease in the Crayola® Model Magic® shaped green bean. Finding trim that resembles broccoli florets at the fabric store helps create the organic shape of broccoli.

Safety Precautions

Always read and follow all manufacturers' instructions.

Ingredients

Tomatoes
Crayola® Model Magic®, white
Rosco® Off Broadway™ Scenic Paint: Fire Red
Rosco® Crystal Gel

Carrots
Crayola® Model Magic®, white
Rosco® Off Broadway™ Scenic Paint: Orange
Rosco® CrystalGel

Green Beans
Crayola® Model Magic®, white
Rosco® Off Broadway™ Scenic Paint: Yellow Ochre, Chrome Oxide Green, Earth Umber

Broccoli
Trim Fringe from Jo-Ann Fabric and Craft Store
Rosco® Off Broadway™ Scenic Paint: Chrome Oxide Green

Lettuce
Bounty® Paper Towels
Rosco® CrystalGel
Rosco® Off Broadway™ Scenic Paint: Yellow Ochre, Chrome Oxide Green, Golden Yellow, and Emerald Green

Tools

- Q-tips® Cotton Swabs
- Metal Ruler
- Scissors
- Hot Glue Gun and Glue Sticks
- Wax Paper
- Paint Brush

Figure 11.1: Cherry tomatoes created from Crayola® Model Magic®

To create the cherry tomatoes, roll pieces of Crayola® Model Magic® into balls ranging in size from a nickel to a quarter. Let harden for at least two hours.

Once the clay is dry, paint with Rosco® Off Broadway™ Fire Red with a Q-tips® Cotton Swab. Since it is challenging to get reds to cover in one coat, you will need to apply at least 2–3 coats of paint so the white of the clay doesn't show through. After that is dry, apply one coat of Rosco® CrystalGel.

To create the baby carrots, roll pieces of Crayola® Model Magic® into small ropes about two inches long. Taper one end of each carrot. Create differing sizes and thicknesses to mimic the variety of baby carrots. Let dry for at least two hours or until the Crayola® Model Magic® begins to stiffen and set. Once the clay is hard, paint with Rosco® Off Broadway™ Orange with a Q-tips® Cotton Swab. This may take a couple of coats until there is no longer white clay showing through the coat of paint. After that is dry, apply one coat of Rosco® CrystalGel or Rosco® Acrylic Gloss. The gloss will create the visual sensation of moisture on the carrots.

To create the green beans, roll pieces of Crayola® Model Magic® into a rope about the thickness and length of a #2 pencil. Using your fingers, create dips in the rope. It will help create the illusion of beans in the pod. Using the edge of a ruler (metal is best, but plastic will do in a pinch), create a centerline in the bean. Taper the ends of each bean.

Let the green beans harden for two hours or until the clay doesn't move when lightly touched. Mix Rosco® Off Broadway™ Yellow Ochre, Chrome Oxide Green, and a little Earth Umber to create the color of green beans. Apply paint with a Q-tips® Cotton Swab. This may take a couple of coats

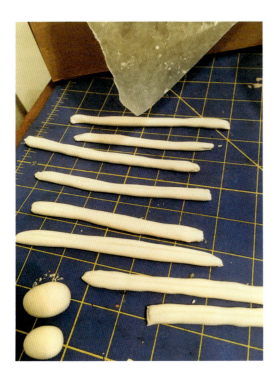

Figure 11.2: Green beans created from Crayola® Model Magic®

Figure 11.3: Painted carrots, tomatoes, and green beans

62 appetizers

Figure 11.4: Fringe for broccoli

Figure 11.5: Fringe cut for broccoli florets

until there is no longer white clay showing through the coat of paint. After that is dry, apply one coat of Rosco® Acrylic Gloss mixed with Flat for a satin finish.

Cut trim from Jo-Ann Fabric and Craft Store into 1" segments. The selvage edge of the trim will become the stalk of the broccoli. Decide on how much stalk is desired, then trim the selvage edge to length. Hot glue at least three sections of trim together to make a broccoli floret. Once the glue has cured, dab Rosco® Off Broadway™ Chrome Oxide Green on the fringe to match research of broccoli.

Create a bed of lettuce on which to place the vegetables by cutting Bounty® Paper Towels into large leaf shapes roughly 5" in diameter. After cutting one shape, stack five or six paper towels, and then cut around the template.

Bare hands work best for this process. Dip two fingers in Rosco® CrystalGel, then coat the paper towel. Be sure the entire surface of the paper towel is covered with Rosco® CrystalGel. Bounty® Paper Towels work well because they are very strong. The paper towels should be at least 50% saturated with CrystalGel. The leaves should still be able to

Figure 11.6: Assembled florets painted

Figure 11.8: Painted paper towels for lettuce

be formed and maintain their shape without having to hold them while they dry. Scrunching up the paper towel is helpful in creating veining and texture quickly. Unfold the paper towel and place on wax paper or a non-stick surface. Shape the leaf-shaped paper towels in slightly cupped shapes. Don't worry about all of the shapes being identical; lettuce off the head is not uniform. Let towels dry for at least 30 minutes.

Use colors similar to those found in your research for lettuce leaves: Rosco® Off Broadway™ Chrome Oxide Green, Yellow Ochre, Golden Yellow, and Emerald Green.

Put about a teaspoon of each color on a palette, dip the brush in each color and mix colors on a palette with a little water to achieve color to match research. Be careful not to use too much water or it will weaken the CrystalGel and you will have flat pieces of lettuce.

On the companion website, there is a recipe for a fruit tray appetizer.

twelve

wonton soup

Salt Dough Time: 10 minutes
Wontons Time: 15 minutes
Broth Time: 10 minutes, cure for 24 hours
Total Time: 35 minutes prep, 24 hours cure

Why This Works—The traditional salt dough recipe has less salt and no vegetable oil or alum. The vegetable oil helps to keep the dough from cracking while rolling it into shape. The alum helps preserve the dough. This salt dough recipe uses much less salt. The dough remains more flexible and stays soft longer while kneading. Heating the ingredients on the stove makes the dough less sticky when rolling it out. In this recipe, a microwave is used to dry the salt dough because wontons are boiled in the soup, not baked or deep-fried.

Smooth-On® Encapso® K is a water clear encapsulation rubber. It is a two-part liquid mixed together in equal parts. It cures to a soft rubber texture. It has a 2-hour pot life and takes 24 hours to cure. Without any colorant, it is as clear as water. It lasts a long time. It is also UV-resistant and easy to color. After it is cured, you can shave the Encapso® K to look like broken glass, diamonds, or ice. While it is still liquid, you can add color to it with Silc Pig® or Ignite® color pigments from Smooth-On®. Encapso® K can be removed by cutting or crumbling it away. If you want to remove it from a glass object, simply coat the glass object in petroleum jelly or Ease Release® 200 before pouring the Encapso® K.

Safety Precautions

Wear gloves and safety glasses when working with Smooth-On® products. Use in a well-ventilated area and avoid directly inhaling mixing agents. Read and follow all manufacturers' instructions.

Ingredients

Salt Dough
2 c. Flour
½ c. Salt
2 c. Water
2 tbsp. Vegetable Oil
4 tbsp. Alum or Cream of Tartar

Wonton Filling
Rosco® Off Broadway™ Scenic Paint: Van Dyke
Rosco® FlexBond or Elmer's® Glue-All®
Sawdust

Broth
Smooth-On® Encapso® K
Smooth-On® Silc Pig® Yellow Concentrated Pigment for Silicone
Thai Unryu Paper: Green

Tools

- Saucepan
- Spoon
- Rolling Pin
- Two Bowls—one for mixing, one for final product
- Ruler
- Knife
- Paper Towel
- Microwave
- Eyedropper
- 12 oz. Plastic Container

66 appetizers

Figure 12.1: The salt dough rolled out and cut into a 4" x 4" square

Figure 12.2: Creating the wonton filling

Figure 12.3: Filling dropped in center of salt dough square

To make the salt dough, mix the dry ingredients in a saucepan. Add water and vegetable oil. Heat over low to medium heat until it is the consistency of mashed potatoes, stirring frequently until there are no more clumps. Stir until the dough forms a ball and pulls away from the sides of the saucepan. Using a plastic spoon, scoop it out on to a lightly floured surface. Knead it until it is smooth and thick. Make a ball. Use immediately or refrigerate in an airtight container. Using a rolling pin, roll dough out so it is less than $\frac{1}{8}$" thick. Cut a 4" x 4" square from the dough.

In a bowl, mix 1 tbsp. of Rosco® FlexBond, 1 tbsp. of sawdust, and ½ tsp. of Van Dyke paint for each wonton. Mix until it reaches the desired consistency. Drop mixture into middle of the dough square.

wonton soup **67**

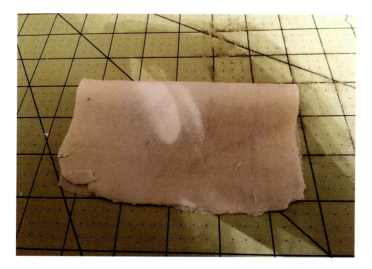

Figure 12.4: Salt dough square folded over filling

Fold dough like a wonton. Check out 10 different ways to fold a wonton at www.homemade-chinese-soups.com/how-to-fold-wontons.html.

Here are two popular options for folding the wonton:

- Option 1: Fold the salt dough in half to create a triangle. Press the edges of the triangle together firmly. Gently fold the two remaining corners around to meet each other.
- Option 2: Fold all four corners of the dough toward the center. Work out any air between the filling and dough. Gather the corners together and gently press to seal.

Once wontons are formed, wrap in a slightly damp paper towel. Place in microwave for 15 seconds to harden. Re-wet the paper towel by pouring water over it and the wonton. Heat in microwave for another 30 seconds. Heating it in the microwave, then wetting it with water and microwaving it again creates the slick wet look of a boiled wonton. Cool and then place in bowl.

In a 12 oz. plastic container, pour equal parts of A and B Smooth-On® Encapso® K to create 8 to 10 oz. of broth. Tint

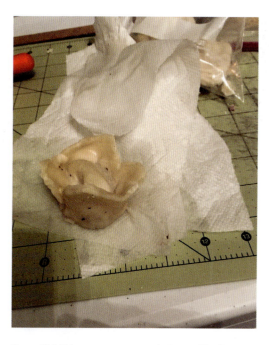

Figure 12.5: Wonton on paper towel after cooking in microwave for an additional 30 seconds

Encapso® K by using an eyedropper to add a tiny amount of Yellow Smooth-On® Silc Pig® Concentrated Pigment. Mix thoroughly.

Pour the Encapso® K in the bowl with the wontons. The wontons will shift as the Encapso® K is added to the bowl and float to the top like actual wontons. As it cures, you can push them further down into the broth. Cut small pieces of green Thai Unryu paper to represent green onion. While the rubber is curing, place the green Thai Unryu paper in the bowl. The green onions can be pushed into the broth as deep as your research indicates. Typically, the green onions tend to float toward the top of the broth. Cure for 24 hours.

68 appetizers

Figure 12.6: Mixing Smooth-On® Encapso® K for broth

Figure 12.7: Completed wonton soup

Section 3
breakfast food

thirteen
doughnuts

72 breakfast food

Total Time: 3 hours

Why This Works—Smooth-On® FlexFoam-iT!® III expands 15 times its initial volume. It rises and cures quickly to a solid flexible foam. Smooth-On® FlexFoam-iT!® III is the lowest density foam and expands the most. Mix ratio is 1:2 Part A to Part B. It has a pot life of 35 seconds and cures in 2 hours.

Smooth-On® FlexFoam-iT!®V is a two-part urethane foam that expands 11 times its initial volume and cures quickly. Mix equal parts by volume. It has a pot life of 50 seconds and cures in 2 hours. Use Ease Release® 2831 to release the urethane foam from most surfaces. Don't use Universal® Mold Release by itself, or any other silicone-based release agents. It will collapse the foam according to the Smooth-On® website. Smooth-On® recommends Universal® Mold Release followed by Ease Release® 2831. If you use a Teflon®-coated doughnut pan, there is no need to use a mold release agent.

Show Application—This recipe could be used for set dressing for *Superior Donuts* by Tracy Letts or any diner show like *Bus Stop* by William Inge or *Spitfire Grill* by James Valcq and Fred Alley.

Safety Precautions

- Wear gloves and safety glasses when working with Smooth-On® products.
- Use in a well-ventilated area and avoid directly inhaling mixing agents.
- Read and follow all manufacturers' instructions.

Ingredients

Smooth-On® FlexFoam-iT!® V
Smooth-On® FlexFoam-iT!® III
Smooth-On® Silc Pig® Brown Concentrated Pigment for Silicone

DAP® Alex Plus® Caulk
Sculpt or Coat®
Rosco® CrystalGel
Sculptural Arts Coating, Inc. Artist's Choice Saturated Scenic Paints™: Raw Umber & Black
Wood Shavings
Design Master® Glossy Wood Tone Spray
Montana™ GOLD Spray Paint: Cream

Tools

- 3 oz. Bathroom Dixie® Cups
- Wilson® Doughnut Pan
- Stirring Stick
- Nitrile or Latex Gloves

Figure 13.1: FlexFoam-iT!® III tinted with Silc Pig® concentrated pigment

The chocolate doughnuts are made by using Smooth-On® FlexFoam-iT!® III. It is a two-part urethane foam. The parts are determined by volume. Measure 1 part Part A and 2 parts Part B into separate plastic containers. Since we only needed a small amount, we used 3 oz. Dixie® Bathroom Cups. The website suggests pre-mixing Part B with a mechanical mixer or drill before adding Part A *into* Part B. Mix for 30 seconds before pouring. Add a small amount of Silc Pig® Brown Concentrated Pigment to the mixture of Parts A and B. Mix vigorously for 30 seconds before pouring. Make sure you stir thoroughly and scrape the sides and bottom of the cup. You need to work quickly because you will only have about 5 more seconds to pour it. The pot life is about 35 seconds. Make sure you stir thoroughly and scrape the sides and bottom of the cup. Pour into the doughnut pan. The foam will be tacky to the touch after 30 minutes and it will be completely set in 2 hours.

The plain cake doughnuts were made by mixing equal parts of FlexFoam-iT!® V. It expands 11 times its initial volume and has a little longer pot life. Smooth-On® FlexFoam-iT!® V is a two-part urethane foam. Mix the parts by volume. Measure equal parts Part A and Part B into separate plastic containers. Since we only needed a small amount, we used 3 oz. Dixie® Bathroom Cups. The website suggests thoroughly pre-mixing (stir or shake) Part A and Part B separately before dispensing. For best results, the manufacturer recommends pre-mixing Part B with a mechanical mixer or drill before adding Part A *into* Part B. Once you add the two parts together, mix quickly and deliberately for a minimum of 15 seconds before pouring. Don't forget to aggressively scrape the sides and bottom several times when you are mixing the parts together. Pour into mold carefully. Don't splash the liquid out of the container. Don't delay between mixing and pouring. These materials cure very quickly. The pot life for this foam is 50 seconds and it will be completely set in 2 hours.

Pour the foam in a Wilson® doughnut pan filling each cavity only ⅛" to ¼" full. The foam will become tacky within 15 minutes. Within 2 hours the foam will be completely cured.

Figure 13.2: FlexFoam-iT!® III tinted with Silc Pig® concentrated pigment and FlexFoam-iT!® V in doughnut pan

Figure 13.3: Cured FlexFoam-iT!® V in doughnut pan

74   breakfast food

Figure 13.4: Cured FlexFoam-iT!® III in doughnut pan

The doughnuts will rise and remain tacky within 15 minutes. After 2 hours, the doughnuts can be removed from the pan.

Once the doughnut is removed from the pan, it can be painted. In a well-ventilated area, spray with a series of Montana™ GOLD Spray Paint in Cream and Design Master® Glossy Wood Tone Spray to match your research of a plain cake doughnut.

Figure 13.5: Cured FlexFoam-iT!® III chocolate doughnuts in pan

Remove the chocolate cake doughnuts from the pan. You will notice the surface of the doughnut is more pockmarked using the FlexFoam-iT!® III than the FlexFoam-iT!® V. This creates an interesting texture that is similar to an actual chocolate cake doughnut.

Remove the chocolate doughnuts from the pan. For a glazed chocolate doughnut, apply a thin layer of Rosco® CrystalGel to the doughnut. The Rosco® CrystalGel mimics glazed icing on doughnuts.

Figure 13.6: Chocolate icing made from Alex Plus® Caulk, Sculpt or Coat®, and scenic paints

For chocolate iced doughnuts, mix DAP® Alex Plus® Caulk and Sculpt or Coat® with raw umber and black Artist's Choice Saturated Scenic Paints™ to create the icing. Mix thoroughly until there is a consistent smooth texture. Frost doughnuts. Wood shavings can be added to look like toasted coconut. The icing dries within 30 minutes depending on humidity.

doughnuts 75

Figure 13.7: Chocolate icing made from Alex Plus® caulking, Sculpt or Coat®, and scenic paints

Figure 13.8: Completed frosted and glazed chocolate doughnuts

fourteen
oatmeal muffins

Total Time: 3 hours

Why This Works—Smooth-On® FlexFoam-iT!® V is a two-part urethane foam that expands 11 times its initial volume and cures quickly. Mix equal parts by volume. It has a pot life of 90 seconds and cures in 2 hours. Use Universal® Mold Release followed by Ease Release® 2831 to release the urethane foam from most surfaces. Don't use Universal® Mold Release by itself, or any other silicone-based release agents. It will collapse the foam according to the Smooth-On® website. If you use a Teflon®-coated muffin pan, there is no need to use a mold release agent.

Show Application—These muffins were created for the University of Cincinnati College-Conservatory of Music's production of *Into the Woods* by Stephen Sondheim and James Lapine. This recipe could be used for set dressing for *Superior Donuts* by Tracy Letts or any diner show like *Bus Stop* by William Inge or *Spitfire Grill* by James Valcq and Fred Alley.

Safety Precautions

- Wear gloves and safety glasses when working with Smooth-On® products.
- Use in a well-ventilated area and avoid directly inhaling mixing agents.
- Read and follow all manufacturers' instructions.

Ingredients

Smooth-On® FlexFoam-iT!® V
Smooth-On® Universal® Mold Release Aerosol Spray and Ease Release® 2831
Bulls Eye® Amber Shellac
Rosco® CrystalGel or Rosco® FlexBond
Design Master® Glossy Wood Tone Spray
Package of Instant Oatmeal

Tools

- 8 oz. Plastic Mixing Cups
- Wilson® Muffin Pan
- Stirring Stick
- Nitrile or Latex Gloves

Figure 14.1: FlexFoam-iT!® V in muffin tin

Spray muffin tin with mold release. Use Universal® Mold Release followed by Ease Release® 2831. If the muffin pan is Teflon®-coated, it won't need mold release.

Smooth-On® FlexFoam-iT!® V is a two-part foam. It was used to create the muffins. Mix the parts by volume. Measure equal parts Part A and Part B into separate plastic containers filling each ⅓ full. The website suggests thoroughly pre-mixing (stir or shake) Part A and Part B separately before dispensing. For best results, the manufacturer recommends pre-mixing Part B with a mechanical mixer or drill before adding Part A *into* Part B. Once you add the two parts together, mix quickly and deliberately for a minimum of 15 seconds before pouring. Don't forget to aggressively scrape the sides and bottom several times when you are mixing the parts together. Pour into mold carefully. Fill each muffin cup at least ¼ full. Don't splash the liquid out of the container. Don't delay between mixing and pouring. These materials cure very quickly. The pot life for this foam is 50 seconds and it will be completely set in 2 hours.

Figure 14.3: Muffins with oatmeal mixture on top

Figure 14.2: FlexFoam-iT!® V muffins removed from tin and coated with shellac

After 40 minutes, the muffins can be removed from the tin. The foam will completely set in 2 hours. After the foam is cured, apply a thin coat of amber shellac to give them a golden baked look. This should be done in a well-ventilated area. Experiment with diluting the amber shellac with denatured alcohol (1:2 shellac to alcohol) to paint the muffin. Build up glazes of amber shellac on the bun. By diluting the amber shellac, you get the color of the amber shellac and by using thinner coats the shellac doesn't build up creating an encapsulated look.

After the shellac has dried, mix a package of instant oatmeal with Rosco® CrystalGel or Rosco® FlexBond. On the top of each muffin, drop a dollop of oat mixture. Smooth it out using your finger or a knife to cover most of the top surface of the muffin. After the oatmeal mixture has dried, apply a thin coat of amber shellac. After the glaze of shellac is dry, create more variation and definition by dusting with Design Master® Glossy Wood Tone Spray.

Figure 14.4: Completed oatmeal muffins

On the companion website, there is a recipe for poppy seed muffins.

fifteen

pancake, bacon, and egg breakfast

Total Time: 5 hours

Why This Works—Smooth-On® FlexFoam-iT!® III expands 15 times its initial volume. It rises and cures quickly to a solid flexible foam. Smooth-On® FlexFoam-iT!® III is the lowest density foam and expands the most. It is important to note that tinted Gel Wax® will bleed into the Smooth-On® Flex-Foam-iT! III if the foam isn't sealed. Use Universal® Mold Release followed by Ease Release® 2831 to release the urethane foam from most surfaces. Don't use Universal® Mold Release by itself, or any other silicone-based release agents. It will collapse the foam according to the Smooth-On® website.

Plastic sheeting, often called by the brand name of Visqueen, is found in the paint area of Lowe's or Home Depot. It comes in different mils or thicknesses. The thicker plastic works better. When the plastic sheeting is carefully heated with a heat gun in a well-ventilated area, it will resemble cooked bacon.

The gel candle wax is tintable, durable, and has a realistic weight for the end product. When crème wax is added to gel wax, it gives the gel wax more structure and reduces the bubbles. The wax will set faster. Both are low-density candle waxes that are long lasting and odorless. Adding a dash of color from the Yaley™ concentrated candle dye to the wax tints the entire wax. All of Yaley's candle dyes are compatible with the gel wax. If the budget is an issue, there has been success in tinting the wax by using crayons.

The GOLD line of Montana™ Spray cans is a high-covering and quick-drying NC-acrylic lacquer. NC-Acrylic lacquer is a solvent-based lacquer with an acrylic resin base combined with a nitrocellulose and alkyd resin. It dries fast because of the rapid evaporation time of the solvent. The BLACK and GOLD lines can be combined. However, Montana GOLD works better on porous surfaces and the Montana BLACK works well on non-porous surfaces. This information is more significant if you are going to be creating murals.

Show Application—This recipe could be used for set dressing for *Superior Donuts* by Tracy Letts or any diner show like *Bus Stop* by William Inge or *Spitfire Grill* by James Valcq and Fred Alley.

Safety Precautions

- Don't pour any wax down the drain.
- Never leave melting wax unattended.
- Use a thermometer to monitor the temperature of the wax.
  - Don't overheat the wax. It will melt around 130°F. The optimum temperature is between 150°F and 170°F. Heat to a maximum of 220°F.
- Keep the wax away from an open flame.
- Always use a potholder when handling a hot pot.
- Always keep an ABC fire extinguisher nearby.
- Wear gloves and safety glasses when working with Smooth-On® products.
  - Use in a well-ventilated area and avoid directly inhaling mixing agents.
- Read and follow all manufacturers' instructions.

Over-Easy Eggs

Ingredients

Smooth-On® FlexFoam-iT!® III
Smooth-On® Universal® Mold Release Aerosol Spray and Ease Release® 2831
Yaley™ Gel Wax®
Yaley™ Brown Concentrated Candle Dye
Yaley™ Yellow Concentrated Candle Dye
Yaley™ White Concentrated Candle Dye
Bulls Eye® Clear Shellac
Bulls Eye® Amber Shellac
Sculptural Arts Coating, Inc. Sculpt or Coat® or Rosco® CrystalGel

Tools

- 3 oz. Bathroom Dixie® Cups
- 6″ Cake pan
- Plastic Egg
- Candle Thermometer

Figure 15.1: Smooth-On® FlexFoam-iT!® III in 6″ cake pan

The egg white is made out of Smooth-On® FlexFoam-iT!® III. Spray the cake pan with Smooth-On® Universal® Mold Release aerosol spray followed by Ease Release® 2831. According to the Smooth-On® website, they caution against using the Universal® Mold Release by itself because it has been known to collapse the foam. They suggest lightly applying the release agent with a soft brush over all surfaces and letting it dry for 30 minutes. Smooth-On® FlexFoam-iT!® III is a two-part foam. Mix the parts by volume. Measure 1 part Part A and 2 parts Part B into separate plastic containers. Since we only needed a small amount, we used 3 oz. Dixie® Bathroom Cups. The website suggests pre-mixing Part B with a mechanical mixer or drill before adding Part A *into* Part B. Mix for 30 seconds before pouring. Pour into 6″ cake pan. Remember you are making over-easy eggs, so the egg white should be an irregular shape. The foam will be tacky to the touch after 30 minutes and it will be completely set in 2 hours.

Figure 15.2: Finished over-easy egg

After the foam is cured, take the egg white out of the pan. Brush amber shellac along the edges of the egg white. This should be a fairly narrow band and can be irregular to simulate the crispy edges of an over-easy egg.

To make the yolk of the egg, melt Gel Wax® in a saucepan on low heat. Add yellow concentrated dye shavings to reach the desired color of an egg yolk. Spray the inside of a plastic egg with Smooth-On® Universal® Mold Release aerosol spray. Check wax temperature with candle thermometer prior to pouring. Pour molten wax into half of a plastic egg and fill it less than halfway to approximate the size of a yolk. To speed up the curing process, place plastic egg with gel wax in freezer.

82   breakfast food

Seal the foam egg white with clear shellac well. If the foam isn't sealed well, the gel wax's color will bleed. Place an egg yolk in the egg white. The yolk can be adhered with a small dab of Sculptural Arts Coating, Inc. Sculpt or Coat®, Rosco® CrystalGel, or DAP® Alex Plus® Caulk. The first two products have the benefit of drying clear.

To give it the appearance of a thin layer of egg white over the yolk and the rest of the egg, melt Gel Wax® in a saucepan on low heat. Add a small amount of white concentrated dye shavings. Pour the molten gel wax over the yolk and egg base.

Pancake, Butter, and Syrup

Ingredients

Smooth-On® FlexFoam-iT!® III
Smooth-On® Universal® Mold Release Aerosol Spray and Ease Release® 2831
Yaley™ Gel Wax®
Yaley™ Brown Concentrated Candle Dye
Sculptural Arts Coating, Inc. Artist's Choice Paints™ or Rosco® Off Broadway™ Scenic Paint: Yellow Ochre, White
Rolyan® Adapt-it® Thermoplastic Pellets or Polly Plastics™ Moldable Plastic Pellets and Color Pellets
Montana™ GOLD Spray Paint in Smash Potato*
Montana™ GOLD Spray Paint in Brown

* When this recipe was created, Montana™ had the color Smash Potato in the GOLD line. It has since been discontinued; however, it is available in the BLACK line (Smash 137's Potato), or the Vanilla in the GOLD line could be substituted.

Tools

- 3 oz. Bathroom Dixie® Cups
- Candle Thermometer

Figure 15.3A: Smooth-On® FlexFoam-iT!® III pancakes

Figure 15.3B: Painted pancakes

The three pancakes are made out of Smooth-On® FlexFoam-iT!® III. Spray three cake pans with Smooth-On® Universal® Mold Release aerosol spray, followed by Ease Release® 2831. According to the Smooth-On® website, they caution against using the Universal® Mold Release by itself because it has been known to collapse the foam. They suggest lightly applying the release agent with a soft brush over all surfaces and letting it dry for 30 minutes. Smooth-On® FlexFoam-iT!® III is a two-part foam. Mix the parts by volume. Since we only needed a small amount, we used 3 oz. Dixie® Bathroom Cups. Measure 1 part (quarter of the Dixie® cup) Part A and 2 parts (half of the Dixie® cup) Part B into separate plastic containers. This amount will make one pancake. The website suggests pre-mixing Part B with a mechanical mixer or drill before adding Part A *into* Part B. Mix for 30 seconds before pouring. Spoon into 6" cake pan. The foam will be tacky to the touch after 30 minutes and it will be completely set in 2 hours.

After the foam is cured, paint the pancakes in a well-ventilated area or under a spray hood; use a light-yellow spray paint like Montana™ GOLD Smash Potato and a brown spray paint to give the pancakes their color. To add a sense of realistic detail from the cooking process, spray Design Master® Glossy Wood Tone around the edges of the pancake where it would brown against the pan.

To make a slice of butter, Adapt-it® moldable thermal plastic was used. Place a small amount of the thermal plastic in hot water. Once it is malleable, form it into a butter pat. Mix yellow ochre and white scenic paints together for the perfect butter color and paint butter pat. Another option would be to melt Polly Plastics™ Moldable Pellets and Color Pellets in a medium saucepan with hot water above 150°F. Once the Moldable Pellets have become clear, take the pellets out of the water. Knead them together to evenly distribute the color and form into a pat of butter. See Fig. 22.6A–D in the Fried Rice recipe on the companion website for more information.

The syrup is made by melting Gel Wax® in a saucepan on low heat. When the wax is melted, add brown concentrated dyes shavings to reach the desired color of the maple syrup. A cheaper alternative to Gel Wax® is to use Elmer's® School Glue Gel and Dr. Ph. Martin's Radiant Concentrated WaterColor. Pour the tinted molten wax (or the glue gel) over the pancakes.

Figure 15.4: Finished pancakes with syrup

Bacon

Ingredients

Plastic Sheeting (4 mil or 6 mil)
DAP® Alex Plus® Caulk
FEV (French Enamel Varnish)
　Bulls Eye® Amber Shellac
　Brown Leather Dye
　Red Leather Dye
　Denatured Alcohol

84 breakfast food

Tools

- Heat Gun

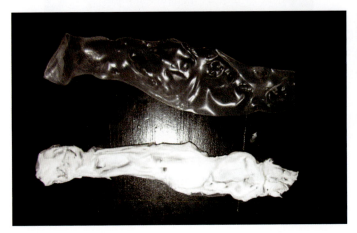

Figure 15.5: Top: strip of plastic sheeting heated by heat gun. Bottom: plastic sheeting coated with DAP® Alex Plus® Caulk

Figure 15.6: Completed bacon

Figure 15.7: Completed pancakes, bacon, and egg

Cut strips of plastic sheeting the size of strips of bacon. Using a heat gun in a well-ventilated area, heat the plastic. Don't get the heat gun too close to the plastic. Move the heat gun slowly over the length of the strip. As the plastic heats up, it will pucker and curl like bacon. Use caution when using the heat gun. The nozzle gets extremely hot.

Let plastic cool once the desired shape is achieved. Coat the plastic in DAP® Alex Plus® Caulk.

Paint the bacon with a series of red and brown FEVs to achieve perfectly cooked bacon strips. FEV stands for French enamel varnish. FEV was originally used in cabinet making for traditional French polishing. It is a completely transparent glaze with a great depth of color. Not only is it transparent, but it is also durable, will seep into crevices and details, and it dries very quickly. To make FEV, mix 1 part shellac to 10 parts denatured alcohol. Add leather dye to reach the desired color. You can use either clear or amber shellac. For this application, it won't affect the color of the FEV.

sixteen
sticky buns

breakfast food

Total Time: 3 hours (30 minutes per mold to cast, 2 hours to cure)

Why This Works—It allows you to buy or make one roll, then create a mold to cast multiple rolls with toppings to suit the show's needs.

Dragon Skin® is a silicone that can be used for a variety of applications from creating skin effects to making a flexible mold. It is both very strong and stretchable. It stretches many times its original size without tearing and will rebound without any distortion. It is also used for medical prosthetics and cushioning.

Dragon Skin® 10 Fast can be tinted by adding Silc Pig® silicone pigments or Cast Magic® effects powders and it can be painted. It is mixed by volume and cures quickly in 75 minutes. Be sure to read all of the manufacturer's directions when using this product. Wear vinyl gloves only when working with this product. Latex gloves will inhibit the curing of the product.

Smooth-On® FlexFoam-iT!® V is a two-part urethane foam that expands 11 times its initial volume and cures quickly. Mix equal parts by volume. It has a pot life of 50 seconds and cures in 2 hours. Use Mann Ease Release® 2831 to release the urethane foam from most surfaces. Don't use Universal® Mold Release or any other silicone-based release agents. It will collapse the foam according to the Smooth-On® website.

Show Application—These sticky buns were built for the University of Cincinnati College-Conservatory of Music's production of *Into the Woods*. This recipe could be used for set dressing for *Superior Donuts* by Tracy Letts or any diner show like *Bus Stop* by William Inge or *Spitfire Grill* by James Valcq and Fred Alley.

Safety Precautions

- When working with Dragon Skin® 10 Fast, make sure you are in a well-ventilated area.
  - Wear safety glasses, long sleeves, and vinyl gloves (not latex gloves) to minimize any contamination to the Dragon Skin®
- Always read and follow the manufacturers' directions.
- Don't pour any wax down the drain.
- Never leave melting wax unattended.
- Use a thermometer to monitor the temperature of the wax.
  - Don't overheat the wax. It will melt around 110°F. The optimum temperature is between 115°F and 120°F. Heat to a maximum of 150°F.
  - Soy wax melts at a lower temperature than other waxes.
- Keep the wax away from an open flame.
- Always use a potholder when handling a hot pot.
- Always keep an ABC fire extinguisher nearby.

Ingredients

Plastic Bread Roll for Casting
Smooth-On® Dragon Skin® 10 Fast
Smooth-On® FlexFoam-iT!® V
Mann Ease Release® 2831 Mold Release
Universal® Mold Release Aerosol Spray
Bulls Eye® Amber Shellac
Design Master® Glossy Wood Tone Spray
Sculptural Arts Coating, Inc. Artist's Choice Saturated Scenic Paints™:
    Burnt Umber
Acrylic Medium
Soy Candle Beads, white and vanilla-scented
Jewelry Beads (to resemble chopped nuts)

Tools

- 18" × 6" Foam-core board to create a box
- Hot Glue Gun
- 8 oz. Plastic Mixing Cups

- Vinyl Gloves
- Stirring Sticks
- Saucepan

Figure 16.1: Purchased plastic roll in mold box

Figure 16.2: Dragon Skin® 10 Fast covering a plastic roll in mold box

½" above the highest point of the plastic roll. It will take 75 minutes for it to fully cure. If it is warmer than 73°F, the working time and cure time will be drastically reduced, according to the Smooth-On® website.

Create a mold box by cutting foam-core board into 4 pieces approximately 3" × 6" for the sides and 1 piece approximately 6" × 6" for the base. Hot glue the pieces together as an open-top box. The box should be 1" to 2" larger than the roll. Hot glue the plastic roll to the bottom of mold box. It is important to glue the object firmly in place before making the mold. It is also important to make sure all seams of the foam board box are sealed completely with a thick bead of hot glue.

Into separate plastic mixing cups, pour equal Parts A and B of Dragon Skin® 10 Fast. Combine Parts A and B into one cup. For 3 minutes, stir thoroughly, making sure you scrape the sides and bottom while stirring. You will only have about 8 minutes to work with this before it begins to set. Pour the mixture in a single spot at the lowest point of the mold. Let the liquid rubber seek its level up and over the roll. A uniform flow will help minimize trapped air. You need to pour at least

Figure 16.3: Dragon Skin® 10 Fast mold filled with FlexFoam-iT!® V

Allow the Dragon Skin® to cure at room temperature before unmolding the plastic bread roll. To remove it from the mold box, cut along the hot-glued corners. Carefully, remove the plastic roll from the mold. Brush the Dragon Skin® mold with Ease Release® 2831 Mold Release. Wait 10 minutes for the Ease Release® 2831 to dry, also known as flash-off, before pouring FlexFoam-iT!® V into the mold.

Smooth-On® FlexFoam-iT!® V is a two-part foam. It was used to create the sticky bun. Mix the parts by volume. Measure equal parts Part A and Part B into separate plastic containers. The website suggests thoroughly pre-mixing (stir or shake) Part A and Part B separately before dispensing. For best results, the manufacturer recommends pre-mixing Part B with a mechanical mixer or drill before adding Part A *into* Part B. Once you add the two parts together, mix quickly and deliberately for a minimum of 15 seconds before pouring. Don't forget to aggressively scrape the sides and bottom several times when you are mixing the parts together. Pour into mold carefully. Don't splash the liquid out of the container. Don't delay between mixing and pouring. These materials cure very quickly. The pot life for this foam is 50 seconds and it will be completely set in 2 hours.

After the foam is cured, take the sticky bun out of the mold. In a well-ventilated area, dilute amber shellac with denatured alcohol (1:2 shellac to alcohol) to paint the sticky bun. Build up glazes of amber shellac on the bun. By diluting the amber shellac, you get the color of the amber shellac and with thinner coats the shellac doesn't build up creating an encapsulated look. After the glazes of shellac are dried, Design Master® Glossy Wood Tone Spray can be sprayed on to create more variation and definition.

Figure 16.5: Painting cinnamon details on sticky bun

To enhance the cinnamon details in the crevices of the sticky bun around the knot, use burnt umber paint mixed with a little acrylic medium. Acrylic medium can be purchased at an art store or use a concentrated scenic medium like Rosco® CrystalGel, Sculpt or Coat®, Rosco® Clear Acrylic Gloss Flat, or Plastic Varnish™. All of the scenic mediums would need to be diluted before mixing with the paint. Acrylic medium creates a transparent glaze by providing additional binder to the diluted pigment of the paint.

Figure 16.4: Unmolded foam sticky bun

sticky buns **89**

Figure 16.6: Painted sticky buns with chopped nuts attached

Hot glue jewelry beads to add chopped nuts to the top of the sticky bun to simulate chopped nuts.

Melt soy candle beads on low in a saucepan. The beads melt faster than regular wax blocks and at a lower temperature. Also, the beads are already white. The vanilla scent is an added bonus; the icing will have a slight lingering scent when dried on the sticky bun.

Figure 16.7A: Melting soy candle beads

Drizzle the melted soy candle wax over the sticky bun. Allow the wax to build up in areas where more icing would pool.

Figure 16.7B: Soy candle wax drizzled on buns for icing glaze

Figure 16.8: Finished sticky bun

Section 4

main entrées and side dishes

seventeen

baked potato with butter and sour cream

Total Prep and Dry Time: 8 hours

Why This Works—Insulation (extruded polystyrene) foam is quite easy to form and cut. It comes in a variety of thicknesses. Buying the contractor pack of ½" thick foam is cost-effective. It can be laminated together with either 3M™ Fastbond™ 30NF Contact Adhesive or Elmer's® Glue-All®. For this recipe, Elmer's® Glue-All® was used. The benefit is this is slightly less expensive and readily available. The foam typically comes in two colors, pink and blue. The pink extruded polystyrene (XPS) is produced by Owens Corning® Foamular® and the blue XPS is produced by Dow™ Styrofoam™.

The gel candle wax is tintable, durable, and has a realistic weight for the end product. When crème wax is added to gel wax, it gives the gel wax more structure and reduces the bubbles. The wax will set faster. Both are low-density candle waxes that are long lasting and odorless. Adding a dash of color from the Yaley™ concentrated candle dye to the wax tints the entire wax. All of Yaley's candle dyes are compatible with the gel wax. If the budget is an issue, there has been success in tinting the wax by using crayons.

To clean up the saucepan, let the gel wax completely cool. It will peel out of the pan.

Polly Plastics™ Moldable Plastic Pellets are easy to use. They melt in hot water (>150°F). They can be manipulated into any shape by hand or by tools. They are also strong and reusable. The pellets can be re-melted many times. It can be painted, drilled, cut, or attached to something else. Polly Plastics™ Moldable Plastic Pellets are clear and can be tinted in an unlimited number of colors by using Polly Plastics™ Color Pellets. The Color Pellets are easy to use and are mess-free. Just drop a few Color Pellets into the hot water (>150°F) with the Moldable Pellets. Once the Moldable Pellets have turned clear, remove from the water and knead the pellets together until the color is evenly distributed. Polly Plastics™ Moldable Plastic Pellets and Color Pellets are inexpensive and readily available on Amazon.com.

Safety Precautions

- Don't pour any wax down the drain.
- Never leave melting wax unattended.
- Use a thermometer to monitor the temperature of the wax.
  - Don't overheat the wax. It will melt around 130°F. The optimum temperature is between 160°F and 170°F. Heat to a maximum of 220°F.
- Keep the wax away from an open flame.
- Always use a potholder when handling a hot pot.
- Always keep an ABC fire extinguisher nearby.
- Read and follow all manufacturers' instructions.

Ingredients

Potato
3 Pieces of 6" × 12" × ¾" Rigid Extruded Polystyrene Foam (commonly known as pink or blue insulation foam)
Elmer's® Glue-All® or 3M™ Fastbond™ Contact Adhesive 30NF
Rosco® FoamCoat or Rosco® FlexBond
Brown Paper Towel
Rosco® CrystalGel
Rosco® Supersaturated™ Scenic Paint: Burnt Umber, Raw Umber
PVC Shavings or Glitter

Sour Cream
2 tbsp. Rosco® CrystalGel
Rosco® Supersaturated™ Scenic Paint: White

Butter
Polly Plastics™ Moldable Plastic Pellets
Polly Plastics™ Color Pellets: Yellow and White

> **Cheese**
> ¼ cup or 3" block of Yaley™ Crème Wax®
>
> To Dye Wax:
> 　　Yaley™ Concentrated Candle Dye—Yellow and Red, or White or Crayola™ Crayon Shavings
> Smooth-On® Universal® Mold Release Aerosol Spray

Tools

- Disposable Roller and Pad or Brush for 3M™ Fastbond™ 30NF
- Nitrile Gloves for 3M™ Fastbond™ 30NF
- Clamps
- Ruler
- Band Saw
  - Eye and Hearing Protection
- Paint Brushes
- G-rasp or Stanley® Surform® Shaver™ or Pocket Plane™
- Dremel® Rotary Tool
- Saucepan
- Spoon
- Candy Thermometer
- A small mold for the wax—shape doesn't matter.

Cut 3 pieces of ¾" XPS foam into 6" × 12" rectangles. Remove the film from each side of the foam. Laminate the pieces together by using either 3M™ Fastbond™ Contact Adhesive 30NF or Elmer's® Glue-All®. This recipe was made with Elmer's® Glue-All®. A lot of glue is needed to laminate the sheets of foam and it needs to be clamped well while it dries so that there is complete contact between each layer of foam and glue.

If 3M™ Fastbond™ Contact Adhesive 30NF is used to adhere the layers, apply a uniform coat of contact adhesive to both surfaces to be laminated together. When the adhesive has dried and is no longer glossy, the pieces can be put together to create a 6" × 12" × 3" block of foam. It will take about 30 minutes for the adhesive to dry. The pieces need to be assembled within 4 hours of the adhesive drying. The longer you wait before assembling the foam, the stronger the bond of the adhesive. Clean up according to package directions.

Once glue has dried, remove the clamps and draw out shapes of potatoes on the foam. One 6" × 12" × 3" piece of foam yields two potatoes.

Use the band saw to cut the potato shapes. Make sure you operate the band saw properly and safely by wearing eye and hearing protection.

Figure 17.1: Shaping with a Dremel® tool

96 main entrées and side dishes

Shape the foam into a potato using a Stanley® Surform® Shaver™ or Pocket Plane™. A Dremel® rotary tool can help shape the foam more quickly or with finer details.

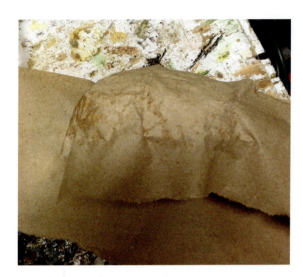

Figure 17.3: Applying a paper towel to the potato

Figure 17.2: Foam coated with Rosco® FlexBond

Figure 17.4: V-shaped notch in the potato, and paper towel trimmed

Coat the potato in either Elmer's® Glue-All®, Rosco® FlexBond™, or Rosco® FoamCoat to seal the foam. To create the skin of the baked potato, glue a brown paper towel to the foam potato. Let dry. Paint the skin to match research image using Rosco® Supersaturated™ Scenic Paint Burnt Umber and Raw Umber or similar acrylic paints.

For a sea-salted skin, add chopped PVC shavings or large white glitter sprinkled over an area coated with glue or CrystalGel. The PVC shavings were the by-product of cutting PVC pipe on the miter saw for another project in the shop.

baked potato with butter and sour cream **97**

Make a V-shaped notch in the foam to replicate how the potato was cut to load the toppings into the potato. Coat the freshly cut foam with FoamCoat then paint to match research of the flesh of a baked potato.

Figure 17.6: Potato with butter

Figure 17.5: Polly Plastics™ Moldable Pellets and Color Pellets

Sour Cream

Mix 2 tbsp. of Rosco® CrystalGel and white Rosco® Supersaturated™ Scenic Paint for sour cream. Drop a dollop on top of the open potato.

Butter

Create butter pat by melting Polly Plastics™ Moldable Pellets in a medium saucepan with hot water above 150°F. Drop 6–10 pellets of white and one pellet of yellow colorant into the pan. Once the Moldable Pellets have become clear, take the pellets out of the water. Knead them together to evenly distribute the color. Form into a small pat of butter. *If the plastic butter comes out too yellow, a glaze of white paint can be applied to match research image.*

Figure 17.7: Baked potato with butter and sour cream

Shredded Cheddar Cheese

Melt ¼ cup or a 3" block of Crème Wax® in a saucepan over medium heat. Add yellow and red concentrated dye to reach the desired color of cheddar cheese. An alternative to using the concentrated candle dye is to use Crayola® crayon shavings to achieve the appropriate cheddar cheese color. Spray your small mold with Universal® Mold Release. Check wax temperature with candle thermometer prior to pouring; it should be 160°F–170°F. Pour molten wax into mold. Once the wax is cooled, remove it from the mold, and grate it with a cheese grater.

Figure 17.9: Shredded tinted Crème Wax® for cheese

Figure 17.8: Tinted Crème Wax® in disposable muffin pan for cheese

eighteen

barbecue ribs with corn on the cob

Total Prep Time: 1 hour
Total Dry Time: 6 hours for curing
Total Time: 7 hours

Why This Works—The benefits for using Smooth-On® products are no scale is necessary; it is a simple 1:1 ratio by volume, and perfect for beginners. The low viscosity of the products offers easy mixing and pouring. Smooth-Cast® 300 has a bright white finish that is durable, paintable, and virtually bubble-free. It captures a tremendous amount of detail. One trial-size kit of Smooth-Cast® 300 could yield at least two dozen bones for the ribs. Smooth-On® Silc Pig® Concentrated Pigment for Silicone can tint the Smooth-Cast® 300. The Silc Pig® is extremely concentrated pigment so use an eyedropper to add the pigment to the Smooth-Cast® 300 a little at a time.

The crème candle wax is tintable and durable, and has a realistic weight for the end product. The wax has more structure, few bubbles, and sets faster than the gel wax. It is a low-density candle wax that is long lasting and odorless. Adding a dash of color from the Yaley™ concentrated candle dye to the wax it tints the entire wax. All of Yaley's candle dyes are compatible with the gel wax. If the budget is an issue, there has been success in tinting the wax by using crayons.

OOMOO® 30 is easy to use, an inexpensive silicone rubber, and cures at room temperature with little shrinkage. The two parts are different colors (Part A is pink, Part B is blue) that make it evident when it is has been stirred thoroughly. It is fairly resistant to tearing and mold degradation when it is used repeatedly for casting.

According to the experts at Smooth-On®, when creating a mold from a model that is porous or organic, the model needs to be sealed with an acrylic spray like Krylon® Crystal Clear Acrylic to prevent failure in the mold process. After it has dried, Mann Ease Release® 200 needs to be applied. Ease Release® 200 is an excellent general-purpose release agent and should be used with silicone molds like OOMOO®.

Safety Precautions

- Wear gloves and safety glasses when working with Smooth-On® products.
  - Use in a well-ventilated area and avoid directly inhaling mixing agents. Read and follow all manufacturers' instructions.
- Don't pour any wax down the drain.
- Never leave melting wax unattended.
- Use a thermometer to monitor the temperature of the wax.
  - Don't overheat the wax. It will melt around 130°F. The optimum temperature is between 160°F and 170°F. Heat to a maximum of 220°F.
- Keep the wax away from an open flame.
- Always use a potholder when handling a hot pot.
- Always keep an ABC fire extinguisher nearby.
- Some liquid latex contains ammonia and its fumes can cause irritation.
  - Be sure to use in a well-ventilated area, avoid eye contact, and read all safety precautions on the label.

Ingredients

Corn on the Cob
Real Corn on the Cob for casting
Krylon® Crystal Clear Acrylic Spray
Smooth-On® OOMOO® 30
Mann Ease Release® 200 Mold Release
3" × 3" block of Yaley™ Crème Wax®
Crayons: Golden Yellow, Yellow, and Brown

BBQ Ribs
Real Rib Bones for casting
Krylon® Crystal Clear Acrylic Spray
Smooth-On® OOMOO® 30
Mann Ease Release® 200 Mold Release

Smooth-On® Smooth-Cast® 300
Smooth-On® Silc Pig® Flesh Concentrated Pigment for Silicone, a smidge
8 pieces 1" × 4" of 1" Rigid Extruded Polystyrene Insulation Foam (commonly known as pink or blue foam)
Kangaroo® Liquid Latex
Rosco® Off Broadway™ Burnt Sienna, Fire Red, Deep Red
Rosco® CrystalGel
Rosco® Clear Acrylic Gloss
Design Master® Glossy Wood Tone Spray

Tools

- 3/16" Foam-core board to create a box
- Utility Knife
- Cutting Mat
- Clear Plastic 8 oz. cups (a larger cup leaves room to stir)
- Rasp
- Small Artist Paint Brushes
- Hot Glue Gun
- Nitrile Gloves
- Safety Glasses
- Saucepan
- Candle Thermometer
- Dremel® Rotary Tool

Corn on the Cob

Purchase an ear of corn. Clean thoroughly and make sure no hair is left on the ear of corn.

Create a mold box by cutting foam-core board in pieces to create a box. The box should be 1" to 2" larger than the ear of corn to be cast. For this project, the box created was 8" × 3" × 6". Hot glue the pieces together as an open-top box. Make sure the seams are completely flush or there is enough

Figure 18.1: Ear of corn in box to be cast

hot glue to make sure none of the liquid OOMOO® 30 will seep out. Taping the outside edges will ensure that all the cracks are covered. The ear of corn needs to be sealed with an acrylic spray like Krylon® Crystal Clear Acrylic to prevent failure in the mold process. Hot glue ear of corn to the bottom of mold box. It is important to glue the object firmly in place before making the mold. Liberally spray the corn and the foam board with Ease Release® 200 Mold Release. Let it dry for at least 5–10 minutes before pouring OOMOO®.

The silicone rubber of OOMOO® 30 will create a negative mold of the corn. Fill half of an 8 oz. plastic cup with Part A. Pour 4 oz. of Part B into the cup with Part A, which should fill the cup. You will have 8 oz. of product that will need to be combined. Using a larger graduated mixing container that is larger than 8 oz. will give you room to mix the two parts. Stir until the pink and blue liquids turn purple. You will have 30 minutes to work with this. If you need more OOMOO® to fill your mold you have time to make more and add it to the mold box. Pour the OOMOO® 30 into the mold box at the lowest point and cover the corn completely including at least 1" above the highest point on the corn so the mold won't break when de-molding it. Allow the OOMOO® 30 to set for 6 hours.

Figure 18.2: Negative mold of ear of corn

To remove the mold from the mold box, cut along the hot-glued corners. Carefully, remove the corn from the mold. You may need to make relief cuts in the OOMOO® around the corn on the cob to remove it because of the shape. Make sure you tape the mold back together before casting the corn. Minimizing or not creating relief cuts is the best option, so the wax doesn't leak out during the casting process. Yaley™ Crème Wax® will be used to create the positive corn on the cob.

Melt a 3" × 3" block of Crème Wax® in a saucepan on medium heat. Use a utility knife to shave pieces off the crayons to create the colorant for the wax. For this project, the colors Golden Yellow, Yellow, and Brown were used. Add the

Figure 18.3: Melting Crème Wax®

wax shavings to the melted Crème Wax® in the saucepan. Stir or swish the gel around to mix the colors thoroughly. Pour a small amount of colored wax out into a ceramic dish to check the color. Repeat until the desired color is achieved. Check wax temperature with candle thermometer prior to pouring.

Figure 18.4: Casting corn on the cob

Before pouring the wax into the mold, make sure it is in a location where it can stay for the next 30 minutes. Pour molten wax into the mold. The mold should not be moved until the wax has hardened which will be at least 30 minutes. Once the wax is cooled, remove it from the mold.

Ribs

An actual rib bone from dinner at Outback Steakhouse® was used for the positive. Thoroughly clean and dry the rib bones. The rib bones need to be sealed with an acrylic spray like Krylon® Crystal Clear Acrylic to prevent failure in the mold process.

Create a mold box by cutting foam-core board in pieces to create a box. The box should be 1" to 2" larger than the rib bones to be cast. For this project, the box created was 4½" × 3" × 2½". Hot glue the pieces together as an open-top box. Make sure the seams are completely flush or there is enough hot glue to make sure none of the liquid OOMOO® 30 will seep out. Taping the outside edges will ensure that all the cracks are covered. Hot glue rib bone(s) to the base of mold box. It is important to glue the object firmly in place before making the mold. Liberally spray the bone(s) and the foam board with Ease Release® 200 Mold Release. Let it dry for at least 5–10 minutes before pouring OOMOO®.

The silicone rubber of OOMOO® 30 will create a negative mold of the rib bone(s). Fill half of an 8 oz. plastic cup with Part A. Pour 4 oz. of Part B into the cup with Part A, which should fill the cup. You will have 8 oz. of product that will need to be combined. Using a larger graduated mixing container that is larger than 8 oz. will give you room to mix the two parts. Stir until the pink and blue liquids turn purple. You will only have 30 minutes to work with this. Pour the OOMOO® 30 into the mold box at the lowest point and cover the rib bones completely including at least ½" to 1" above the highest point on the rib bone(s) so the mold won't break when de-molding it. Allow the OOMOO® 30 to set for 6 hours.

Figure 18.5: Part A and Part B of OOMOO® mixed in plastic cup

Figure 18.6: Smooth-Cast® 300 Parts A & B measured out in plastic cups

104   main entrées and side dishes

Figure 18.7: Negative mold of rib bone filled with Smooth-Cast® 300

Figure 18.8: Unmolded ribs

De-mold the rib bone from the cured OOMOO® 30. Spray the negative mold with Ease Release® 200. Let it dry for at least 5 minutes and spray another coat of mold release. Let dry for at least another 5 minutes before pouring the mold.

Smooth-Cast® 300 uses equal parts of Part A and Part B. Pour ½" of Part A into a mixing plastic mixing container, followed by ½" of Part B into a separate container so you can accurately assess that you have equal parts. Combine into a single cup and stir thoroughly. It has a pot life of 3 minutes. The clear liquid can be tinted with Smooth-On® Silc Pig® Flesh Concentrated Pigment for Silicone. Add it by eyedropper to the liquid and stir thoroughly. Pour the liquid into the mold. The liquid will turn white (or the tinted color) as it cures. The rib bone will be ready to be removed from the mold in 15 minutes. Note the mold becomes hot because Smooth-Cast® 300 generates heat as it cures. Wear gloves. Repeat. Typically, there are 14 ribs for a full slab of pork ribs.

Create the meat portion of the ribs by cutting XPS (extruded polystyrene foam) insulation foam. Shape the eight pieces of 1" × 4" × 1" foam using a rasp. Use a Dremel® rotary tool to create a cavity for each bone. Glue cast bone into the cavity with low-temperature hot glue. Let dry for about 20 minutes.

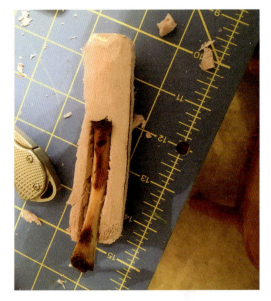

Figure 18.9: XPS foam cavity for rib bone

Coat the foam with Kangaroo® Liquid Latex to create texture of cooked ribs. Create the outer crust of the ribs by applying about ¼" thick Rosco® CrystalGel mixed with Rosco® Off Broadway™ paints. Create tinted Rosco® CrystalGel for the ribs to match research—grilled, smoked, or with extra barbecue sauce. For this project, Rosco® Off Broadway™ colors of Burnt Sienna with a little of Fire Red and Deep Red were used. Let dry. Darken the ends of the bones with paint to appear charred.

Figure 18.11: Painted ribs

Spray with Design Master® Glossy Wood Tone Spray. Coat the ribs with a coat of Rosco® Clear Acrylic Gloss transparent glaze.

Figure 18.10: Process of painting ribs

nineteen

chef salad

Total Prep Time: 4 hours
Lettuce:
Prep: 1 hour
Painting: 30 minutes
Drying time: 30 minutes (depending on weather, or use of hair dryer)
Meat: 10 minutes
Cheese: 20–30 minutes (depending on cooling time of wax)
Hard-boiled Eggs: 30–45 minutes (two-step process)
Total Time: 3½–4 hours (depending on dry time)

Why This Works—Creating small lettuce leaves from a ribbed white toilet tissue like Cottonelle® saturated with Rosco® CrystalGel works well because the toilet paper has a similar thickness as lettuce. The ribbed nature of Cottonelle® creates a similar texture to lettuce veining. Mixing Rosco® Crystal-Gel with paint or ink dye reduces the opportunity to damage the leaf-shaped toilet tissue. It can be shaped and molded to resemble lettuce leaves. Leaves can be cut by using scissors or X-acto® knife. Scissors tend to work better since the leaves don't have to be precise, just similar in shape.

The gel candle wax is tintable and durable, and has a realistic weight for the end product. When crème wax is added to gel wax, it gives the gel wax more structure and reduces the bubbles. The wax will set faster. Both are low-density candle waxes that are long lasting and are odorless. Adding a dash of color from the Yaley™ concentrated candle dye to the wax tints the entire wax. All of Yaley's candle dyes are compatible with the gel wax. If the budget is an issue, there has been success in tinting the wax by using crayons.

Adding more crème wax to the gel wax allows the gel wax to set faster, but it can be harder to cut once it has hardened. For a softer cheese, use a 2:1 ratio of gel wax to crème wax.

Safety Precautions

- Follow all manufacturers' instructions on each product.
- Don't pour molten wax down the drain.
- Always keep an ABC fire extinguisher nearby.
- Never leave melting wax unattended.
- Use a thermometer to monitor temperature of wax.
- Keep wax away from an open flame.
- Always use a potholder when handling a hot pot.
- Don't overheat the wax. Heat to a maximum of 220°F.

Ingredients

Lettuce
Cottonelle® Toilet Paper
Lettuce Leaf Templates
Rosco® CrystalGel
Rosco® Off Broadway™ Scenic Paint: Yellow Ochre, Chrome Oxide Green, Golden Yellow, and Emerald Green

Meat
Turkey—scraps of Beige Silk Lining from Club Sandwich*
Ham—scraps of Pink Corduroy, reverse side from Club Sandwich*
* The club sandwich recipe is in Chapter 21.

Tomatoes
Crayola® Model Magic®, white
Rosco® Off Broadway™ Scenic Paint: Fire Red
Rosco® CrystalGel

Cheese
3" block of Yaley™ Crème Wax®
Yaley™ Yellow Concentrated Candle Dye or yellow crayon shavings
Yaley™ Red Concentrated Candle Dye or orange crayon shavings
Smooth-On Universal® Mold Release

Hard-Boiled Eggs
Yaley™ Gel Wax®
Yaley™ White Concentrated Candle Dye or white crayon shavings
Crayola® Model Magic®, white

108 main entrées and side dishes

Tools

- Scissors or X-acto® Knife
- Pencil or Sharpie®
- Mixing Container
- Wax Paper
- Q-tips® Cotton Swabs
- Candle Thermometer
- Cheese Grater
- Saucepan
- Spoon
- Aluminum muffin tin for the mold
- Plastic Easter Eggs
- Paint Brush
- Paint Palette
- Snap-Off Blade Utility Knife
- Hair Dryer, optional

Do a Google Images search for "lettuce leaf template." There is a variety of options. For this project, a felt leaf template called "gratitude felt leaves" from www.sawyoo.com was used. Print out the template. If the image is too small when printed, the template can be imported into Adobe Photoshop to enlarge the image from 4½" × 5 ⅞" to 7" × 9". Another method of enlarging the template would be to photocopy it at 156%.

Fold the toilet paper at least three or four times to reduce the number of leaves you need to trace. Use a pencil or Sharpie® to trace a variety of leaf templates on the toilet paper. The ridges inherent in the Cottonelle® toilet paper mimic the veins and texture of lettuce. For one salad, about 1 to 1½ cups of lettuce will be needed. Make extra leaves in case some don't turn out exactly as desired.

Cut out the leaves using scissors or an X-acto® knife. Precision is not necessary, there can be differences in the leaves, since the leaves only need to be similar in shape.

Dip two fingers in Rosco® CrystalGel, then coat the toilet paper. Be sure to get the entire surface of the toilet paper covered with Rosco® CrystalGel. It should be completely

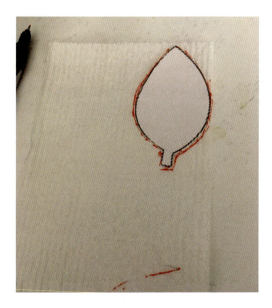

Figure 19.1: Tracing the leaf template on toilet paper

Figure 19.2: Toilet paper leaves coated with in Rosco® CrystalGel and shaped

chef salad 109

Figure 19.3: Painted lettuce leaves

Figure 19.4: Strips of fabric for diced ham and turkey

saturated. Pinch the paper leaves to create the center stem of the leaf. Place on wax paper or a non-stick surface. Don't worry about all of the shapes being uniform, as lettuce off the head is not uniform. Let leaves dry for at least 30 minutes or use a hair dryer to speed up the drying time.

Put about a teaspoon of each of the following colors on a palette—Rosco® Off Broadway™ Chrome Oxide Green, Yellow Ochre, Golden Yellow, Emerald Green, and CrystalGel. Mix the colors together to match research image. Add a small amount of Rosco® CrystalGel and a little water to each color to create a translucent glaze to paint each lettuce leaf. Be careful not to use too much water or it will dissolve the CrystalGel and you will have flat pieces of lettuce. Adding CrystalGel into the color will help alleviate this issue. Let dry on wax paper.

The meat was created using scraps of materials used in the club sandwich recipe. Light beige silk lining resembles turkey lunchmeat. The reverse side of pink corduroy simulates ham. For each fabric, cut into ½" × 3" strips then cut the strips into ¼" × ½" pieces. Sprinkle the ham and turkey pieces on the lettuce.

To create the cherry tomatoes, roll pieces of Crayola® Model Magic® into balls ranging in size from a nickel to a quarter. Let harden for at least two hours.

Once the clay is dry, paint with Rosco® Off Broadway™ Fire Red with a Q-tips® Cotton Swab. Since it is challenging to get reds to cover in one coat, you will need to apply at least 2–3 coats of paint so the white of the clay doesn't show through. After that is dry, apply one coat of Rosco® CrystalGel.

110 main entrées and side dishes

Figure 19.5: Painted cherry tomatoes

Figure 19.6: Wax in mold for shredding cheese

Figure 19.7: Wax shredded for cheese

Melt a 3″ block of Yaley™ Crème Wax® in a saucepan on medium. Add yellow and red concentrated dye to reach the desired color of cheddar cheese. An alternative to using the concentrated candle dye is to use Crayola® crayon shavings to achieve the appropriate cheddar cheese color. Spray Universal® Mold Release on one or two compartments of the muffin tin for your mold. Check wax temperature with candle thermometer prior to pouring. Pour molten wax into mold. Once the wax is cooled, remove it from the mold, and grate it with a cheese grater. For this example, the leftover cheese block created for the baked potato recipe was used. Use a cheese grater to grate the cheese over the assembled salad.

Melt 2 teaspoons of Yaley™ Gel Wax® in a saucepan on medium. Add white Crayola® crayon shavings. After the Gel

chef salad   **111**

Figure 19.8: Creating the hard-boiled eggs in bottom half of plastic Easter egg mold

Wax® is the correct color, pour it into the bottom half of each of the Easter eggs. A muffin tin, box, or egg crate can hold the plastic eggs upright while the wax is poured and cools.

Make nickel or quarter sized balls of Crayola® Model Magic® for the yolks. Submerge them into the Gel Wax® before it cools.

Once wax has cooled, remove the wax egg from the plastic Easter egg. It should just pop out of the plastic egg with a little pressure flexing to break the seal of the wax with the plastic. Slice the egg into wedges or slices with a snap-off utility knife (run blade under hot water) or hot knife to make clean cuts through the wax. Place egg on top of the salad.

Figure 19.9: Completed chef salad

twenty

chicken lo mein

Noodles: 10 minutes
Chicken: 10 minutes
Total Time: 20 minutes prep, overnight to 24 hours to dry

Why This Works—Noodles are easily replicated by cutting cotton yarn, a string mop, or cotton sash cord/clothesline into lengths for noodles and dipping them into brewed black tea or a mixture of Dr. Ph. Martin's® Bombay™ India Ink Brown and water. After experimenting with both options, it seemed as though the tea dyeing the string was more successful.

According to the product information, the benefit of using Rosco™ Premiere Clear is that it is an advanced water-based urethane that is suitable for sealing and protecting finishes, floors, and high traffic surfaces. It is long lasting, durable, and hard, and is resistant to abrasion coating, as well as being environmentally safe and VOC compliant.

Traditional edible lo mein recipes have a variety of vegetables—onion or green onion, cabbage, celery, carrot, bok choy, mushrooms, peas, and broccoli—many of which are created in other recipes in this book.

For this recipe, regular latex house paint was used to paint the chicken because it was on hand in the shop.

Safety Precautions

- Always read and follow all manufacturers' directions.
- Always double-check the SDS (Safety Data Sheets) for each product used and make sure the components of the product are not harmful. Companies often change the chemical makeup of their products over the years; don't assume that by checking once that the product is safe, it will always be safe.

Ingredients

Chicken
Crayola® Model Magic®, white
Valspar® Touch of Tan V090-2 or Rosco® Off Broadway™ Scenic Paint: White and Yellow Ochre
¼ c. Rosco® Premiere Clear Water Based Polyurethane Gloss

Noodles and Vegetables
Cotton Sash Cord/Clothesline, Tubular Cotton Yarn or String Cut in 10" lengths
Dr. Ph. Martin's® Bombay™ India Ink Brown or Black Tea
Thai Unryu Paper: Green and Orange

Tools

- Medium Saucepan
- Paint Brushes
- Mixing Containers, Small

Figure 20.1: Crayola® Model Magic® rolled out

114   main entrées and side dishes

Figure 20.2: Crayola® Model Magic® cut into strips for chicken

Roll out Crayola® Model Magic® in an ⅛" thick disk. Cut into small strips for chicken. Paint with a glaze of Valspar® Touch of Tan or Rosco® Off Broadway™ White and Yellow Ochre mixed with Rosco® Premiere Clear. Let dry.

Figure 20.3: Cutting yarn into lengths

Figure 20.4: Noodles ready to dye

For the noodles, cut yarn into 12" to 16" lengths. Mix two drops of Dr. Ph. Martin's® Bombay™ India Ink Brown with two cups of water in a mixing container. Mix thoroughly to avoid getting blotches on the noodles. In batches of 20–25 strands, dip the yarn into the ink-water mixture. Wring out the excess water so the noodles will dry quicker. *(An alternative, which worked as successfully, is to make an 8 oz. cup of black tea. Use lukewarm water to avoid burning your hand. Once tea has brewed to desired darkness, dip the noodles into the tea. Use a pencil or dowel rod to push the noodles in the tea. Once the noodles are fully saturated, place the noodles in a Ziploc® bag to squeeze out the excess liquid from the noodles.)* Place noodles on a plate and let dry for 15 minutes.

chicken lo mein   **115**

Figure 20.5: Chicken and noodles ready for dyeing

Mix one drop of Dr. Ph. Martin's® Bombay™ India Ink Brown with one cup of water in a mixing container. Do a test first, to make sure you have the color you want. Pour over the chicken pieces. Let dry.

Arrange the chicken strips on plate and adjust the noodles around them. Cut pieces of green and orange Thai Unryu paper. The paper will create the strips of carrots, bok choy leaves, and peas. Dip the paper into the same ink/tea and water mixture as the chicken. Arrange the "vegetables" in the chicken and noodles. Mix equal parts, about 1½ tbsp. each, of water and Rosco® Premiere Clear Water Based Polyurethane Gloss. Pour over the noodles and let dry for 24 hours.

On the companion website, there is a recipe for Chinese Chicken (Sesame Chicken or General Tso's Chicken) and Fried Rice.

Figure 20.6: Dye for chicken and noodles

Figure 20.7: Chicken and lo mein noodles on plate after dyeing

Figure 20.8: Chicken lo mein finished

twenty one

club sandwich

main entrées and side dishes

Total Prep and Dry Time: 6 hours

Why This Works—The gel candle wax is tintable, durable, and has a realistic weight for the end product. When crème wax is added to gel wax, it gives the gel wax more structure and reduces the bubbles. The wax will set faster. Both are low-density candle waxes that are long lasting and are odorless. For the budget conscious, wax crayons have been successful in tinting the wax. Another option is to use the Yaley™ concentrated candle dye to tint the entire wax. All of Yaley's candle dyes are compatible with the gel wax.

Using fabric for lunchmeat and other sandwich ingredients is cost-effective. For this project, ⅛ of a yard of fabric was purchased as well as a yard of trim for the lettuce and bacon, and a small piece of upholstery foam for approximately $10.50.

Safety Precautions

- Don't pour any wax down the drain.
- Never leave melting wax unattended.
- Use a thermometer to monitor the temperature of the wax.
  - Don't overheat the wax. It will melt around 130°F. The optimum temperature is between 160°F and 170°F. Heat to a maximum of 220°F.
- Keep the wax away from an open flame.
- Always use a potholder when handling a hot pot.
- Always keep an ABC fire extinguisher nearby.
- Read and follow all manufacturers' instructions.

Ingredients

Bread
15" × 17" piece of 1" High Density Polyurethane Foam (commonly known as upholstery foam)
Rosco® Supersaturated™ Scenic Paint: White, Burnt Umber, Yellow Ochre, Burnt Sienna
Design Master® Glossy Wood Tone Spray Paint

Meats
Ham:
⅛ yard of Pink Corduroy, reverse side

Turkey:
⅛ yard of Beige Silk Lining

Bacon:
½ yard Ruffle Trim
Rosco® Supersaturated™ Scenic Paint: White, Burnt Umber, Yellow Ochre, Burnt Sienna
Design Master® Glossy Wood Tone Spray Paint

Lettuce:
½ yard Ruffle Trim

Mayonnaise:
Rosco® CrystalGel
Rosco® Supersaturated™ Scenic Paint: White, Yellow Ochre

Tomato:
Yaley™ Gel Wax®
Yaley™ Crème Wax®
Red Crayon
Smooth-On® Universal® Mold Release aerosol spray
Rosco® Supersaturated™ Scenic Paint: White, Burnt Umber, Yellow Ochre, Burnt Sienna

Tools

- Scissors
- Ruler
- 4" Diameter Circle Cookie Cutter
- Candle Thermometer
- Ceramic Mold (a shallow round dish like a ramekin)
- Saucepan
- Spoon
- Knife

club sandwich **119**

Using a 4" diameter circle cookie cutter, draw at least 6 circles on both the pink corduroy and the silk lining. Cut out. The color of the fabric can be modified with acrylic scenic paint or by using Design Master® Glossy Wood Tone Spray Paint as desired.

Cut 4" × 4" squares of foam for the bread slices. Each sandwich will need 1½ squares. Cut the squares diagonally to create two triangle pieces. The 1" foam is too thick for a club sandwich. Cut the thickness in half to create slices ½" thick. Each sandwich will use 6 triangles of foam.

Dip the bread slices in an off-white paint diluted with water to match white bread. Paint edges of foam to look like

Figure 21.1: Fabrics and trims purchased at fabric store

Figure 21.2: Drawing a circle on beige lining

Figure 21.3A: Cutting Upholstery Foam

120 main entrées and side dishes

Figure 21.3B: Painting the crust on the bread

Figure 21.4: Ruffle trim for lettuce

crust with a light brown to match research. Dust the tops of foam with Design Master® Glossy Wood Tone Spray Paint in a well-ventilated area or under a spray hood. This will make the bread look toasted.

Cut the green ruffle trim into 3″ lengths for the lettuce. Color can be adjusted with paint as desired.

Figure 21.5A: Melting wax for tomato

Melt equal parts of both Gel Wax® and Crème Wax® in a saucepan on low heat. Use a utility knife to create shavings of red crayon to color the wax. Add to the saucepan until the desired color is achieved. Spray the ramekin with Universal® Mold Release. Check wax temperature with candle thermometer prior to pouring. Pour molten wax into a round, ceramic baking dish. Only about ⅛″ is needed in the mold to simulate a slice of tomato. Once the wax is cooled, remove it from the mold. Cut in half with a knife.

club sandwich   **121**

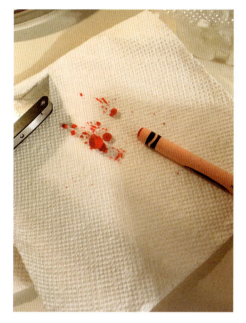
Figure 21.5B: Red crayon shavings for coloring wax

Figure 21.5C: Melted wax in mold for tomato

Figure 21.6: Completed bacon

First, cut the seam allowance side off the ruffle trim to create the bacon. Mix Rosco® Supersaturated™ Scenic Paint White, a little Burnt Umber and Yellow Ochre to base the fabric for the fatty portion of the bacon. It might take two coats. Paint both sides. Mix Rosco® Supersaturated™ Scenic Paint Burnt Sienna and Burnt Umber for the meat portion of bacon. Paint each strip of fabric to match research. Rosco® CrystalGel tinted with Burnt Umber or Design Master® Glossy Wood Tone spray paint could be used to finish the bacon painting to the desired visual crispness.

Create mayonnaise by mixing Rosco® CrystalGel with white and yellow ochre paint to match research image of mayonnaise. Line up your triangle slices of bread on the work surface. Two slices of bread will be the top pieces, two slices will be middle slices, and the last two will be the bottom slices of bread. Use the mayonnaise-colored Rosco® CrystalGel to adhere the ingredients to pieces of bread.

Figure 21.7: Mayonnaise on bread

122   main entrées and side dishes

The assembly of this sandwich is upside down and will be turned right side up at the end. Stack lettuce, a slice of tomato, bacon, turkey (loosely fold the circle in half), and ham (loosely fold the circle in half) on top of the two slices of bread. Repeat for the middle two slices of bread. Use the mayonnaise-colored Rosco® CrystalGel to adhere the top of the middle slice of bread stack to the ham of the stack on the top slice of bread. Then adhere the bottom slice of bread to the top of the assembled sandwich. Flip the entire sandwich over. Additional details to add could include securing a frill pick or cocktail sword to the top of the bread slice.

Figure 21.8: Completed club sandwich

twenty two
hanging meats

Total Prep Time: 3½ hours (Salami: 75 minutes; Pepper Meat: 75 minutes; Sausage: 40–50 minutes)
Total Painting Time: 1–2 hours
Total Dry Time: 1–2 hours
Total Time: 5–8 hours

Why This Works—Meat netting can be purchased online at a variety of sources including Amazon.com. For less than $20, an assortment of sizes, colors, and styles can be purchased on Amazon.com, ranging from 3" to 11½" diamond patterns for meats and 1" in diameter for large turkeys or hams.

Sausage links can be created in many ways. This recipe creates a longer link of sausage similar to a kielbasa from backer rod. Backer rod is a low-density polyethylene foam and is commonly referred to as ethafoam in the theatre and entertainment industry. Ethafoam® is a trademarked product from the Sealed Air Company. If shorter links of sausage are needed, upholstery polyurethane foam or batting in panty hose could be used.

Safety Precautions

- Always read and follow all manufacturers' directions.
- Always double-check the SDS (Safety Data Sheets) for each product used and make sure the components of the product are not harmful. Companies often change the chemical makeup of their products over the years; don't assume that by checking once that the product is safe, it will always be safe.
- Always wear appropriate personal protection equipment when working with power tools.
- Some liquid latex contains ammonia and the fumes can cause irritation.
  - Be sure to use in a well-ventilated area, avoid eye contact, and read all safety precautions on the label.
  - According to the label of the Kangaroo® Liquid Latex, it does not contain ammonia.

Ingredients

Salami #1 (with Mold Casing)
3 pieces 2" × 18" × 1" Rigid Extruded Polystyrene Foam (commonly known as pink or blue insulation foam)
Titebond® Wood Glue
Meat Netting and Twine
Rosco® Off Broadway™ Scenic Paint: Earth Umber, Raw Sienna, Red
Baby Powder
Rosco® Premiere Clear Water Based Polyurethane or Rosco® Clear Acrylic Flat
Design Master® Glossy Wood Tone Spray for additional toning, if desired.

Salami #2
3 pieces 2½" × 18" × 1" Rigid Extruded Polystyrene Foam (commonly known as pink or blue insulation foam)
Titebond® Wood Glue
Kangaroo® Liquid Latex
Meat Netting and Twine
Rosco® Off Broadway™ Scenic Paint: Earth Umber, Raw Sienna, Red
Rosco® Premiere Clear Water Based Polyurethane or Rosco® Clear Acrylic Flat
Design Master® Glossy Wood Tone Spray for additional toning, if desired.

Peppered Salami
3 pieces 3" × 22" × 1" Rigid Extruded Polystyrene Foam (commonly known as pink or blue insulation foam)
Titebond® Wood Glue
Rosco® FlexBond or Elmer's® Glue-All®
Saw Dust
Rosco® Off Broadway™ Scenic Paint: Earth Umber,
Americana® Red Barn Satin Multi-Surface Acrylic Paint
Rosco® Premiere Clear Water Based Polyurethane or Rosco® Clear Acrylic Gloss

Minwax® Wood Finish™ Stain, Special Walnut
Design Master® Glossy Wood Tone Spray
Light Gray spray paint

Sausage
1¼" Diameter Backer Rod (also known as Ethafoam®)
String
Rosco® FlexCoat
Rosco® Off Broadway™ Scenic Paint: Earth Umber, Raw Sienna
Rosco® Clear Acrylic Gloss
Design Master® Glossy Wood Tone Spray

Tools

- C-Clamps
- Band Saw
- Palm or Orbital Sander
- Japanese Ryoba Saw
- Stanley® Surform® Shaver™ or Pocket Plane™ or Sandpaper
- Paint Brush
- Small Containers to Mix Paint

For a salami with a mold casing, cut three pieces of 2" × 18" × 1" Rigid Extruded Polystyrene Foam (commonly known as pink or blue insulation foam). Laminate the pieces together using a generous amount of Titebond® Wood Glue (or any foam adhesive) spread evenly on the foam. Place a larger piece of lauan or similar wood on either side of the foam between the clamps to distribute the pressure of clamps to avoid crushing the foam. Clamp tightly with C-clamps or bar clamps. Let the glue dry 30–40 minutes.

Remove the clamps after the glue is completely dry. Cartoon the desired shape of the salami based on the research images. Use a Japanese Ryoba saw or band saw to cut out the shape. Shape the salami using a palm or orbital sander.

To create the dark reddish brown of the cured salami casing, mix Rosco® Off Broadway™ Earth Umber, Raw Sienna, and Red. *If the salami isn't going to be handled a lot, painting directly on the foam will save time. If it is going to be highly interactive, the foam needs to be primed with products like Rosco® CrystalGel, FoamCoat, FlexCoat, FlexBond, or Sculpt or Coat®. These products adhere to the foam and will reduce the likelihood of the paint flaking off.* Let the paint dry, coat with Rosco® Clear Acrylic Gloss. If additional toning is needed, use Design Master® Glossy Wood Tone Spray.

Figure 22.1: Coating salami with baby powder to create the mold casing

To simulate the mold, which helps with the aging process on the casing of certain meats, coat with baby powder while the acrylic gloss is still wet. Seal with at least one coat of Rosco® Premiere Clear Water Based Polyurethane or Rosco® Clear Acrylic Flat.

Cut a 24" length of meat netting. Slide foam salami in the tube of netting. Tie ends with twine and trim excess netting.

For a salami without a mold casing, cut three pieces of 2½" × 18" × 1" Rigid Extruded Polystyrene Foam (commonly

Figure 22.3: Completed salami with mold casing in meat netting

known as pink or blue insulation foam). Laminate the pieces together using a generous amount of Titebond® Wood Glue (or any foam adhesive) spread evenly on the foam. Place a larger piece of lauan or similar wood on either side of the foam between the clamps to distribute the pressure of clamps to avoid crushing the foam. Clamp tightly with C-clamps or bar clamps. Let the glue dry 30–40 minutes.

Remove the clamps after the glue is completely dry. Cartoon the desired shape of the salami based on the research images. Use a Japanese Ryoba saw or band saw to cut out the shape. Shape the salami using a palm or orbital sander.

Coat foam in Kangaroo® Liquid Latex and let it dry.

To create the dark reddish brown of the cured salami casing, mix Rosco® Off Broadway™ Earth Umber, Raw Sienna, and Red. Let the paint dry, coat with Rosco® Premiere Clear Water Based Polyurethane or Rosco® Clear Acrylic Flat.

If additional toning is needed, use Design Master® Glossy Wood Tone Spray.

Cut a 24" length of meat netting. Slide foam salami in the tube of netting. Tie ends with twine and trim excess netting.

Figure 22.2: Tying meat netting

hanging meats **127**

Figure 22.4: Coating the foam with saw dust

Figure 22.5: Completed peppered meat sliced on cutting board

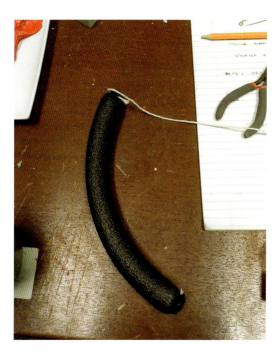

Figure 22.6: Backer rod end tied with twine

To create the peppered meat-like salami, cut three pieces of 3″ × 22″ × 1″ Rigid Extruded Polystyrene Foam (commonly known as pink or blue insulation foam). Laminate the pieces together using a generous amount of Titebond® Wood Glue (or any foam adhesive) spread evenly on the foam. Place a larger piece of lauan or similar wood on either side of the foam between the clamps to distribute the pressure of clamps to avoid crushing the foam. Clamp tightly with C-clamps or bar clamps. Let the glue dry 30–40 minutes.

Remove the clamps after the glue is completely dry. Cartoon the desired shape of the peppered meat based on the research images. Use a Japanese Ryoba saw or band saw to cut out the shape. Shape the meat using a palm or orbital sander.

Paint meat shape with Rosco® Off Broadway™ Earth Umber, then let dry. Coat the painted foam with thin layer of Rosco® FlexBond. Roll the foam meat in a bed of sawdust. Let glue and saw dust dry for 30–45 minutes.

Using a paint brush, paint the sawdust with Minwax® Special Walnut Wood Finish™ stain in a well-ventilated area. After the stain is dry (4–6 hours), mist with Design Master® Glossy Wood Tone Spray and light gray spray paint to match research of peppered salami. *To finish this in a more expedient manner, the sawdust can be toned with Design Master® Glossy Wood Tone Spray and black spray paint to match research.* Let dry, then seal with Rosco® Premiere Clear Water Based Polyurethane or Rosco® Clear Acrylic Gloss.

Cut a 24″ length of meat netting. Slide foam salami in the tube of netting. Tie ends with twine and trim excess netting or slice and paint the medallions of meat as shown in Figure 22.6. Dilute Americana® Red Barn Satin Multi-Surface Acrylic Paint with an equal part of water and brush on the slices. Seal with Rosco® Premiere Clear Water Based Polyurethane or Rosco® Clear Acrylic.

For the sausage, cut a couple of lengths of 1¼″ backer rod, one that is long enough to bend in half to create a loop and one that is about 9″ long.

The backer rod needs to be primed with Rosco® FlexCoat. Other products like Rosco® CrystalGel, FoamCoat, FlexBond, or Sculpt or Coat® will also work. These products adhere to the foam and will reduce the likelihood of the paint flaking off.

Mix a base color to match the research using Rosco® Off Broadway™ Scenic Paint Raw Sienna and Earth Umber for basecoat.

Mist with Design Master® Glossy Wood Tone Spray to tone the sausages to match research. After that is dry, apply a coat of Rosco® Acrylic Gloss.

Figure 22.7: Finished painted sausage

twenty three
honey-glazed ham

Total Time: 4 hours

Why This Works—The trick to making any paint treatment look like a realistic object is multiple layers of translucent glazes. Starting with pink extruded foam reduces the need for a base coat. The variety of types of glazes—FEV, Glossy Wood Tone, and scenic paint—create a convincing honey-glazed ham.

Tip: Even though 3M™ Fastbond™ Contact Adhesive 30NF is water-soluble, using disposable brushes or rollers is helpful. If you have multiple projects to work on, you can put your Fastbond® brush or roller in a plastic bag to keep it from drying out and use it later in the day.

Safety Precautions

- The Safety Data Sheet recommends using gloves when working with 3M™ Fastbond™ Contact Adhesive 30NF.
- This brand of liquid latex contains ammonia and can cause irritation. Be sure to use in a well-ventilated area, avoid eye contact, and read all safety precautions on the label.

Ingredients

3 pieces of 5" × 6" × 2" Rigid Extruded Polystyrene Foam (commonly known as pink or blue insulation foam)
3M™ Fastbond™ Contact Adhesive 30NF
1" O.D. PVC Pipe, Short Length ≤ 5"
Rosco® CrystalGel
Castin'Craft® Mold Builder Liquid Latex Rubber
Rosco® Supersaturated™ Scenic Paints
Design Master® Glossy Wood Tone Spray
FEV (French Enamel Varnish):
   Bulls Eye® Amber Shellac
   Brown Leather Dye
   Denatured Alcohol

Tools

- Disposable Roller and Pad or Brush for 3M™ Fastbond™ 30NF
- Nitrile Gloves for 3M™ Fastbond™ 30NF
- 1" Spade Bit
- Drill
- Japanese Ryoba Saw
- Band saw
- Dremel® Tool with small engraving bit
- Hot Glue Gun and Glue
- PaintBrushes

Apply a uniform coat of Fastbond™ 30NF to both surfaces to be laminated together. When the adhesive has dried and is no longer glossy, the pieces can be put together to create a 6" × 5" × 6" block of foam. It will take about 30 minutes for the adhesive to dry. The pieces need to be assembled within 4 hours of the adhesive drying. The longer you wait before assembling the foam, the stronger the bond of the adhesive. Clean up according to package directions.

Figure 23.1: Laminated XPS foam for ham

Shape the foam to resemble a ham using a band saw and Japanese Ryoba saw.

Figure 23.2: Foam shaped

Use a Dremel® tool with a small engraving bit to make the scored crosshatched skin. Once the foam is shaped, coat in a layer of burnt sienna paint. Seal the foam with Rosco® CrystalGel.

Figure 23.3: Hole created for 1" PVC tubing to be inserted for a hambone

Drill a hole in the foam for a small section 1" diameter PVC tube to be inserted for the hambone. The length of PVC tube should be no longer than two inches. Use a hot glue gun to adhere the PVC tube in the hole. Coat the foam and PVC in another layer of Rosco® CrystalGel.

Figure 23.4: Ham coated in two layers of liquid latex

Once Rosco® CrystalGel has cured, apply two layers of liquid latex. The layers of latex will replicate the fat on the ham. Apply a glob of latex to cover the end of the PVC bone. Let it dry.

Coat the rind of the ham in FEV. FEV stands for French enamel varnish. FEV was originally used in cabinet making for traditional French polishing. It is a completely transparent glaze with a great depth of color. Not only is it transparent, but it is also durable, will seep into crevices and details, and it dries very quickly. To make FEV, mix 1 part shellac to 10 parts denatured alcohol. Add leather dye to reach the desired color. You can use either clear or amber shellac. It won't affect the color of the FEV.

Make candied brown sugar by mixing sawdust into Rosco® CrystalGel. Apply directly to the ham. Once it is dry, spray Design Master® Glossy Wood Tone on the sawdust in a well-ventilated area or under a spray hood.

Figure 23.5: Ham coated in FEV and sawdust sugar

Paint the fleshy interior of the ham using brilliant red, burnt sienna, white, and neutral base Rosco® Supersaturated™ Scenic Paints. Let dry. Apply a coat of amber shellac. Let dry. Coat in a layer of Rosco® CrystalGel.

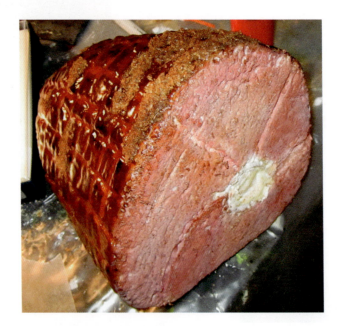

Figure 23.6: Painted ham

twenty four

lettuce wraps

Total Time: 2–3 hours (depending on dry time)

Why This Works—Creating large lettuce leaves from a strong, white (no inked patterns is helpful) paper towel like Bounty® Paper Towels saturated with Rosco® CrystalGel works well because the paper towels are a similar thickness as lettuce. Once the Rosco® CrystalGel is applied to paper towel, balling the paper towel up ensures that it gets evenly coated and produces a texture simulating the veining of the leaf. It can be shaped and molded to resemble a lettuce leaf.

By using a muffin tin, multiple mounds of the meat filling can be created and cured at the same time.

Safety Precautions
Follow all manufacturers' instructions on each product.

Ingredients

Lettuce
Bounty® Paper Towels
Rosco® CrystalGel
Rosco® Off Broadway™ Scenic Paint: Yellow Ochre, Chrome Oxide Green, Golden Yellow, and Emerald Green

Meat Filling
Packing Peanuts
Rosco® RoBo Glue or Elmer's® Glue-All®
Rosco® Off Broadway™ Scenic Paint: Raw Umber
Rosco® Acrylic Gloss
Rosco® CrystalGel

Tools
- Scissors
- Mixing Container
- Muffin Tin
- Spoon
- Wax Paper
- Palette
- Paint Brush

Cut Bounty® Paper Towels into large leaf shapes roughly 5" in diameter. After cutting one shape, stack five or six paper towels, and then cut around the template.

Figure 24.1: Paper towels shaped with Rosco® CrystalGel

Dip two fingers in Rosco® CrystalGel, then coat the paper towel. Be sure to get the entire surface of the paper towel covered with Rosco® CrystalGel. Balling up the paper towel is helpful as it creates veining and texture. Unfold the paper towel and place on wax paper or a non-stick surface. Shape the leaf-shaped paper towels in slightly cupped shapes. Don't worry about all of the shapes being uniform as lettuce off the head is not uniform. Let leaves dry for at least 30 minutes.

Using similar colors as the lettuce leaves in the chef salad recipe, Rosco® Off Broadway™ Chrome Oxide Green, Yellow Ochre, Golden Yellow, and Emerald Green, put about a teaspoon of each color on a palette. Dip the brush in each color and mix colors on a palette with a little water to achieve color to match research. Be careful not to use too much water or it will dissolve the Rosco® CrystalGel and you will have flat pieces of lettuce if the first coat of Rosco® CrystalGel isn't fully cured, which takes 24 hours.

Break up packing peanuts into small pieces. Place inside a mixing container. Pour Rosco® RoBo Glue or Elmer's® Glue-All® on top of peanuts. Spoon a small amount into a muffin tin for six muffins.

Mix Rosco® Off Broadway™ Scenic Paint—Raw Umber and Rosco® Acrylic Gloss for a slightly opaque translucent glaze and paint the meat mixture. Let dry. After the paint is dry, place a mound of meat filling in the center of each lettuce leaf. Use Rosco® CrystalGel to adhere the meat filling to the lettuce leaf and to wrap the leaf around the filling. Let dry. Once it is completely dry, place on plate.

Figure 24.2: Meat mixture in muffin tin

Figure 24.3: Painted meat filling assembled in lettuce wrap

136 main entrées and side dishes

Figure 24.4: Completed lettuce wraps

twenty five

lobster tail

Total Prep Time: 30 minutes
Total Dry Time: 1½ hours for curing (24–72 hours for a full cure)
Total Time: 2 hours (24–72 hours for a full cure)

Why This Works—There are several ways to obtain a positive model to create a mold in order to cast the lobster tail: purchasing a plastic lobster (12″ × 6″ × 2″) on Amazon.com (for about $6); purchasing a lobster at a local supermarket for roughly $15; going to a restaurant, ordering a lobster tail (at Outback Steakhouse® for $10.99 or one of the best specimens can be found at The Melting Pot® for $37.95 as part of a four-course meal), and bringing the shell home—freeze the shell upon returning from the restaurant so it doesn't spoil or degrade. Casting and molding a real cooked lobster tail is too fragile. Ultimately, the best and most economical way is to start with a plastic lobster.

Safety Precautions

Read and follow all manufacturers' instructions.

Show Application—This recipe could be used for *Tribes* by Nina Raine.

Ingredients

Plastic Lobster for casting
2 oz. Crayola® Model Magic®, white
Rosco® Off Broadway™ Scenic Paint: Orange, Fire Red, Brilliant Red, and Burnt Sienna
Rosco® Clear Acrylic Gloss

Tools

- Dremel® Tool
- Utility Knife or X-acto® Knife
- Cutting Mat
- Small Artist Paint Brushes
- Safety Glasses
- Dremel® Rotary Tool with sanding bit

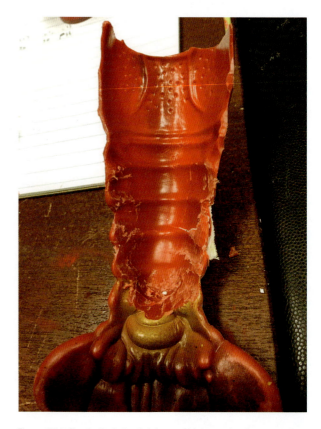

Figure 25.1: Top half of plastic lobster with extra plastic removed

lobster tail **139**

Figure 25.2: Lobster tail shell in box to be cast

Figure 25.3: Unmolded lobster shell

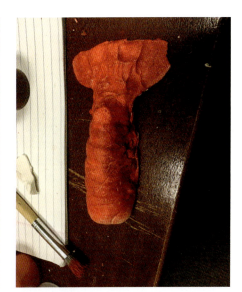

Figure 25.4: Base paint on lobster shell

Using the utility knife, cut the head off the plastic lobster. Split the body in half length-wise. Since the lobster is hollow, once the first cut is made, it is easy to remove excess plastic. Remove all the superfluous plastic on inside of the tail, leaving the tail fins. Use a Dremel® rotary tool with sanding bit to smooth out the rough edges of the plastic.

Press about 2 oz. of Crayola® Model Magic® into the plastic lobster shell. *One 8 oz. bag of Crayola® Model Magic® will make 4 lobster tails.* Make sure the Crayola® Model Magic® covers the entire tail fin. Allow the clay to harden for at least 30 minutes. Slowly and carefully remove the modeling clay from the shell. Since the clay won't be fully cured, it might break or tear.

After the tails have cured for a minimum of 90 minutes, the exterior of the clay will be hard enough to paint.

Use a scumble technique to paint the shell with Rosco® Off Broadway™ Fire Red, Orange, and Burnt Sienna to match research image.

Figure 25.5: Details painted on lobster tail

Once the first layer of paint has dried, stipple Rosco® Off Broadway™ Brilliant Red. Use Burnt Sienna to add shadows and details to the articulating pieces of the shell and tail. After the paint dries, coat it with Rosco® Clear Acrylic Gloss.

Repeat the process of pressing Crayola® Model Magic® into the plastic lobster shell. In Fig. 25.7, the Crayola® Model Magic® covers the entire tail fin; the Model Magic® fin can be cut off for the meat. Allow the clay to harden for at least 30 minutes. Slowly and carefully remove the modeling clay from the shell. Since the clay won't be fully cured, it might break or tear.

After the meat has cured for about 45 minutes, the exterior of the clay will be hard enough to paint, but not solidly cured. Stipple and dry brush the ridges of the abdomen with Rosco® Off Broadway™ Fire Red and Orange.

Use an X-acto® knife or utility knife to split the top while the clay is still pliable to push it together to create the split-top that would happen during the cooking process.

Figure 25.6: Casting lobster meat

Figure 25.7: Painting lobster meat

Figure 25.8: Plated completed lobster tail and meat

twenty six

pierogi

Prep Time: 30 minutes
Total Dry Time: Salt Dough: 15 minutes/24 hours; **Shellac:** 15–45 minutes

Why This Works—The traditional salt dough recipe has less salt and no vegetable oil or alum. The vegetable oil and alum help to keep the dough from cracking while rolling it into shape. This salt dough recipe uses one less cup of salt. The dough remains more flexible and stays soft longer while kneading. Heating the ingredients on the stove makes the dough less sticky when rolling it out.

Show Application—This recipe could be used for Anton Chekhov's *The Three Sisters*.

Safety Precautions

Always read and follow all manufacturers' instructions.

Ingredients

Salt Dough
2 c. Flour
1 c. Salt
1 c. Water
2 tbsp. Vegetable Oil
2 tbsp. Alum
Rosco® Supersaturated™ Scenic Paint: Burnt Sienna
Bulls Eye® Clear Shellac

Tools

- Saucepan
- Spoon
- Rolling Pin
- Ruler
- 4" Diameter Circle Cookie Cutter
- Rounded (scalloped) Clay Modeling Tool

To make the salt dough, mix the dry ingredients in a saucepan. Add water and vegetable oil. Heat over low heat until it is the consistency of mashed potatoes, stirring until there are no more clumps. This takes about 8 minutes. Using a plastic spoon, scoop it out on to a lightly floured surface. Knead it until it is smooth and thick. Make a ball about the size of a racket ball. Use immediately or refrigerate in an airtight container. Using a rolling pin, roll out the dough on a lightly floured surface. Roll until it is no more than ⅛" thick. The dough should be thin. Using the 4" circle cutter, cut out circles of dough. Using the excess dough, create a small ball no bigger than a super-high bounce ball, about 1" in diameter.

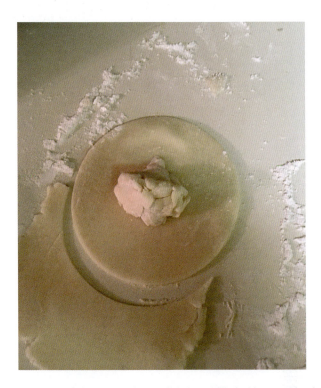

Figure 26.1: Salt dough cut into a 4" circle and filled with excess dough

Figure 26.2: Sealing pierogi with modeling tool

Figure 26.3: Pierogi air-drying

Place the dough ball in the center of the 4" circle of dough. Fold dough in half around filling. Use a scalloped-clay modeling tool or crimp by hand to seal outside edge.

Let air-dry overnight. If you need to speed up the drying process, you could microwave them for 15 seconds.

Coat dried pierogies with Bulls Eye® Clear Shellac. To create the pan-seared coloring on the pierogies, use Burnt Sienna Rosco® Supersaturated™ Scenic Paint or similar acrylic paint.

twenty seven

roast beef with mashed potatoes and gravy

Total Time: 8 hours

Why This Works—Insulation (extruded polystyrene) foam is quite easy to form and cut. It comes in a variety of thicknesses. It does come in contractor packs of ½" thick foam, but for this project getting the 1" foam will produce a better result. It typically comes in two colors, pink and blue. The pink extruded polystyrene (XPS) is produced by Owens Corning® Foamular® and the blue XPS is produced by Dow™ Styrofoam™. If the foam is going to be handled a lot, you may want to make sure the paint adheres well to the foam by coating the foam first with either Rosco® FoamCoat, CrystalGel, or 3M™ Fastbond™ Contact Adhesive 30NF before painting. Each of those products bonds better with the foam and helps the paint not flake off.

For this recipe, a previously constructed small ham from a production of *The Best Christmas Pageant Ever* was recycled to create roast beef. It was constructed by laminating five layers of rigid extruded polystyrene foam, which were approximately 4" × 6" and then were shaped into the form of a small boneless ham. The original ham was created in less than three hours with dry time. Repurposing food props is a time-efficient approach to create a new item.

The traditional salt dough recipe has less salt and no vegetable oil or alum. The vegetable oil and alum (or cream of tartar, in a pinch) help to keep the dough from cracking while rolling it into shape. Heating the ingredients on the stove makes the dough less sticky when rolling it out. In this recipe, the alum was omitted because the salt dough was going to be sealed shortly after it was made. Alum not only makes the dough more elastic, but also acts as a preservative if all of the dough isn't sealed.

The gel candle wax is tintable and durable, and has a realistic weight for the end product. It is a low-density candle wax and is both long lasting and odorless. It can be colored by adding a dash of color from the Yaley™ concentrated candle dye to the wax. The dye will color the entire wax. All of Yaley's candle dyes are compatible with the gel wax. If the budget is an issue, there has been success in tinting the wax by using crayons.

Safety Precautions

- Always read and follow all manufacturers' directions.
- Don't pour any wax down the drain.
- Never leave melting wax unattended.
- Use a thermometer to monitor the temperature of the wax.
  - Don't overheat the wax. It will melt around 130°F. The optimum temperature is between 160°F and 170°F. Heat to a maximum of 220°F.
- Keep the wax away from an open flame.
- Always use a potholder when handling a hot pot.
- Always keep an ABC fire extinguisher nearby.

Ingredients

Roast Beef
¼" to ½" slices of Rigid Extruded Polystyrene Insulation Foam (commonly known as pink foam)
Rosco® Off Broadway™ Scenic Paints: Earth Umber
Rosco® CrystalGel

Mashed Potatoes
Half a batch of Salt Dough as follows:
    1 c. Flour
    1 c. Salt
    1 c. Water
    1 tbsp. Vegetable Oil
Rosco® Off Broadway™ Scenic Paints: White
Rosco® Scenic Paints: Acrylic Gloss

Gravy
Yaley™ Gel Wax®
Brown Crayon

main entrées and side dishes

Tools

- Hand Rasps
- Hacksaw
- Saucepan
- Spoon
- Paint Brush
- Small Mixing Container
- Wax Paper

To recreate the foam roast, laminate five layers of rigid extruded polystyrene foam (approximately 4" × 6"), then shape into the form of a small meat roast.

Slice foam with a hacksaw into ¼"–½" slices.

Use a hand rasp to shape the surface of the slices. A rasp will create a rough meat-like texture to the slice of foam as well as camouflage the lamination of layers.

Paint edges of foam slices with undiluted Rosco® Off Broadway™ Earth Umber to simulate a browned and caramelized roast beef. For the interior meat, use Rosco® Off Broadway™ Earth Umber diluted as a wash. An easy method is to load the paint brush with Earth Umber, then dip the brush into water, and finally apply the slightly diluted paint to the pink foam. By using pink foam as the base and a glaze of earth umber, it recreates the warm tinges of roast beef as a red meat. Once paint has dried, coat in Rosco® CrystalGel to give it a little sheen like a juicy slice of roast beef.

Make a batch of salt dough by mixing the dry ingredients in a saucepan. Add water and vegetable oil. Heat over low heat until it is the consistency of mashed potatoes, stirring until there are no more lumps.

Spoon the desired helping of the salt dough on to wax paper on a plate. Use the spoon to create ridges and texture in the salt dough. Create a paint wash using Rosco® Off Broadway™

Figure 27.1: Slicing foam with a hacksaw

Figure 27.2: Slices of foam for roast beef

Figure 27.3: Shaping the foam with a rasp

roast beef with mashed potatoes and gravy   **147**

Figure 27.4: Painted foam slices for roast beef

Figure 27.5: Salt dough mashed potatoes on wax paper being painted.

Figure 27.6: Meat and potatoes on plate

White (or any other acrylic or latex white paint) and water to match your research. After paint has dried, seal with a coat of Rosco® Acrylic Gloss. Let dry completely.

Melt 1 cup of Gel Wax® in a saucepan on medium heat. Create shavings or small shards of brown crayon to color Gel Wax®. Mix crayon into Gel Wax® and stir until completely incorporated. To check the color of the Gel Wax®, pour a small sample out into a pan or dish. Add more color shavings to achieve the desired color of gravy based on research.

Once potatoes are dry, slip the potatoes off the wax paper on to the plate. Arrange the meat slices on plate and secure. Ladle melted wax gravy on to plate.

Figure 27.7: Completed roast beef, mashed potatoes, and gravy on plate

twenty eight

salmon fillet with side salad

Total Time: 3 hours

Why This Works—Creative Paperclay® can be sculpted, molded, or shaped while it is moist. It air-dries to a hard finish that can be sanded or carved. It is odorless and easy to use. It can be painted or water-based paint can be kneaded into the Paperclay® while it is moist. Paperclay® will generally dry overnight, depending on room temperature and humidity. According to the Paperclay® website, if you are in a hurry, unpainted projects can be dried in a 250°F oven for 30 minutes or until dry.

Safety Precautions

- Don't pour any wax down the drain.
- Never leave melting wax unattended.
- Use a thermometer to monitor the temperature of the wax.
  - Don't overheat the wax. It will melt around 130°F. The optimum temperature is between 160°F and 170°F. Heat to a maximum of 220°F.
- Keep the wax away from an open flame.
- Always use a potholder when handling a hot pot.
- Always keep an ABC fire extinguisher nearby.
- Always read and follow all manufacturers' instructions.

Show Application—This dish was built for University of Cincinnati College-Conservatory of Music's production of *Don Giovanni*. It was used in the banquet scene in Act I. The actors pretended to eat them.

Ingredients

Salmon Fillet
Paperclay®
Acrylic Paints (coral, pink, white)
Clay Molding Tools
Bulls Eye® Clear Shellac

Side Salad
Tissue Paper: 3 different shades of green, 1 purple
Sculpt or Coat®
Yaley™ Gel Wax®
Yaley™ Crème Wax®
Yaley™ Red Concentrated Candle Dye
Orange Poppy Silk Flower Petals
White Seed Beads
Design Master® Glossy Wood Tone Spray
Design Master® Spray Paint, Almond or Off-White
Balsa Wood, 1/16" × 3" × 18" strip

Tools

- Saucepan
- Candle Thermometer
- Scissors
- Cutting Mat

Figure 28.1: Paperclay® formed into a salmon fillet

Follow the package instructions on the Paperclay® to form a 2" × 4" salmon fillet. For your working surface, you will want a plastic surface to prevent sticking. You can use a cutting mat, a piece of plastic wrap, or a piece of a trash bag. Wax paper works but isn't as durable. Looking at your research image, you will notice that it isn't a uniform cuboid. A sculpting tool was used to form the detailed grain of the fillet. Let the Paperclay® dry. This could take a day or so depending on room temperature or humidity. You can speed up the drying process by popping it in the oven at 250°F for approximately 30 minutes.

Using acrylics paints, paint the fillet referring to your research image. You will want to mix some light coral, pink, and darker corals. Apply a layer of clear shellac to seal the finished salmon fillet.

Side Salad

Tear tissue paper into small lettuce shapes. Use three shades of green for the variation of lettuce leaves. Dip each piece of tissue paper into Sculpt or Coat®. Roll the paper in your fingers and then pull it apart. This process will give the tissue paper the texture and ribs of lettuce. Repeat process with purple tissue paper to represent purple cabbage. Additional colors of tissue paper could be used to be mesclun or red leaf lettuce in the salad. Create shredded carrots by plucking a few petals off of orange poppy silk flowers and use scissors or a matte knife to cut slivers off the petals.

Figure 28.2: Painted salmon fillet

Figure 28.3: Detail of tissue paper for lettuce and shredded flower petals for carrots

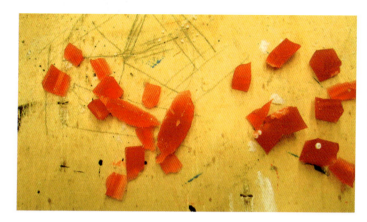

Figure 28.4: Diced tomatoes made from Gel Wax®

Figure 28.5: Detail of side salad with purple cabbage and almonds added

Melt 2 parts Gel Wax® and 1 part Crème Wax® in a saucepan on low heat. Once wax is completely melted, add red candle dye colorant shavings to tint to the desired color of tomatoes. The mold can be any ceramic or metal pan or plate since this method is to create diced tomatoes. Spray your mold with Universal® Mold Release. Pour into mold. Sprinkle a few white seed beads into wax to resemble seeds. Wax will set in 2 hours. Remove from the mold and dice into small cubes (or whatever shape you desire) with a regular knife. *This method could be used to make colored peppers, or change the shape of the mold to create tomato wedges.*

In a well-ventilated area or under a spray hood, tone the dried tissue paper lettuce leaves with Design Master® Glossy Wood Tone Spray Paint and almond-colored spray paint. This process will create a more realistic look to the lettuce.

Cut the shape of almond slices out of the balsa wood strip. Paint the edges of the almonds with umber paint. Lightly dry brush the tops of the almonds with umber. If you would like to add cheese to the side salad, use one of the cheese recipes and grate it on top. To secure the side salad to the plate, Sculpt or Coat® was used. CrystalGel® could be used to give the lettuce a little more of a crisp look with a bit of a sheen as if the salad had a vinaigrette dressing.

Figure 28.6: Plated salmon fillets and salad

twenty nine

spinach quiche

Total Time: 3 hours

Why This Works—The traditional salt dough recipe has less salt and no vegetable oil or alum. The vegetable oil and alum help to keep the dough from cracking while rolling it into shape. Heating the ingredients on the stove makes the dough less sticky when rolling it out.

The gel candle wax is tintable and durable, and has a realistic weight for the end product. When crème wax is added to gel wax, it gives the gel wax more structure and reduces the bubbles. The wax will set faster. Both are low-density candle waxes that are long lasting and are odorless. Adding a dash of color from the Yaley™ concentrated candle dye to the wax tints the entire wax. All of Yaley's™ candle dyes are compatible with the gel wax. If the budget is an issue, there has been success in tinting the wax by using crayons.

Adding more crème wax to the gel wax allows the gel wax to set faster, but it can be harder to cut once it has hardened. For a softer quiche, use a 2:1 ratio of gel wax to crème wax.

Safety Precautions

- Don't pour any wax down the drain.
- Never leave melting wax unattended.
- Use a thermometer to monitor the temperature of the wax.
  - Don't overheat the wax. It will melt around 130°F. The optimum temperature is between 160°F and 170°F. Heat to a maximum of 220°F.
- Keep the wax away from an open flame.
- Always use a potholder when handling a hot pot.
- Always keep an ABC fire extinguisher nearby.
- Always read and follow all manufacturers' instructions.

Ingredients

Salt Dough
2 c. Flour
2 c. Salt
1 c. Water
2 tbsp. Vegetable Oil
2 tbsp. Alum
PAM® Cooking Spray
Thai Unryu Paper (8½" × 11" sheets): Green, Light Yellow
Spray Paint: hunter green
Yaley™ Gel Wax®
Yaley™ Yellow Concentrated Candle Dye
Yaley™ White Concentrated Candle Dye
Bulls Eye® Amber Shellac

Tools

- 9" Tart Plate
- Rolling Pin
- Saucepan
- Candle Thermometer

Figure 29.1: The salt dough crust after baking

154 main entrées and side dishes

Preheat oven to 350°F. Spray the tart pan with PAM® cooking spray. To make the salt dough, mix the dry ingredients in a saucepan. Add water and vegetable oil. Heat over low heat until it is the consistency of mashed potatoes, stirring until there are no more clumps. Using a plastic spoon, scoop it out on to a lightly floured surface. Knead it until it is smooth and thick. Make a ball. Using a rolling pin, roll dough out so it is less than 1/8" thick. Place the dough in tart plate, pressing it into the bottom. Bake at 350°F for 20 minutes. Once the crust has cooled, remove it from the tart pan and coat it with amber shellac to give it a golden brown color.

Figure 29.3: Torn Thai Unryu paper: (left) original color, (right) paper spray painted hunter green

Figure 29.2: Gel Wax® with dye melting in pan

Melt a 4" × 4" block of Gel Wax® in a saucepan on low heat to create the savory custard filling. Add yellow and white concentrated dye shavings to reach the desired color of egg custard.

Create the spinach by tearing pieces of green Thai Unryu paper. In a well-ventilated area or under a spray hood, spray the green Thai Unryu paper hunter green to better match the color of spinach, if needed. Although it isn't pictured, a lighter yellow paper was torn to represent other ingredients like onions and cheese.

Figure 29.4: Gel Wax® filling and paper spinach in salt dough crust

Once the correct color is achieved for the Gel Wax®, carefully pour the melted wax into the crust. While the filling is beginning to cool, place the spinach and onion pieces in the wax. You will want some of the spinach to be submerged in the filling.

After the wax has cooled completely, coat the filling with a layer of amber shellac. The amber shellac adds the final touch of realism giving the impression of the release of the oils and browning that would occur during the baking process.

Figure 29.5: Completed quiche

thirty

turkey

Foam Laminating Time: 24–36 hours
Shaping Time: 2½ hours
Painting and Coating: 2–3 hours including dry time
Total Time: 30–42 hours

Why This Works—The trick to making any paint treatment look like a realistic object is multiple layers of translucent glazes. Starting with pink extruded foam reduces the need for a base coat. The variety of types of glazes—FEV, Glossy Wood Tone, and scenic paint—creates a convincing roasted turkey.

Insulation (extruded polystyrene) foam is quite easy to form and cut. It comes in a variety of thicknesses. It does come in contractor packs of ½" thick foam, but for this project getting the 1" foam will produce a better result. It typically comes in two colors, pink and blue. The pink extruded polystyrene (XPS) is produced by Owens Corning® Foamular® and the blue XPS is produced by Dow™ Styrofoam™. If the foam is going to be handled a lot, you may want to make sure the paint adheres well to the foam by coating the foam first with either Rosco® FoamCoat, CrystalGel, or 3M™ Fastbond™ Contact Adhesive 30NF before painting. Each of these products will bond with the foam allowing additional layers of paint not to flake off the foam.

There are a few options for laminating the polystyrene foam. Rosco® FlexBond, Elmer's® Glue-All®, Titebond®. Wood Glue, and 3M™ Super 77™ Classic or 78™ Spray Adhesive will all work. It is important to note that 3M™ changed the formula for Super 77™ and it now has acetone in it. Acetone will "eat" the polystyrene foam. The classic formula doesn't "eat" the foam. 3M™ has developed Polystyrene Insulation 78™ Spray Adhesive that can safely be used to adhere polystyrene foam together. Both of these spray adhesives create a stronger bond if you spray both surfaces to be laminated together and let them tack up for a minimum of 30 seconds before bonding the two surfaces together.

Tip: After using any aerosol adhesive (or paint), invert the can and depress the spray tip until the spray is free of adhesive (or paint). By adopting this practice, the spray tip will not clog as frequently.

If Rosco® FlexBond, Elmer's® Glue-All, or Titebond® Wood Glue are used, after the layers are laminated, make sure you apply enough weight on the pieces while they are drying. Using a ratchet strap will apply a substantial amount of pressure, but make sure the edges are protected from the straps cutting into the foam by adding wood blocks under the straps.

Safety Precautions

- Always read and follow all manufacturers' directions.
- Always double-check the SDS (Safety Data Sheets) for each product used and make sure the components of the product are not harmful. Companies often change the chemical makeup of their products over the years; don't assume that by checking once that the product is safe, it will always be safe.
- Always wear appropriate personal protection equipment when working with power tools.
- Some liquid latex contains ammonia and its fumes can cause irritation.
  - Be sure to use in a well-ventilated area, avoid eye contact, and read all safety precautions on the label.

Ingredients

5 pieces of 12" × 18" × 1" Rigid Extruded Polystyrene Foam (commonly known as pink or blue insulation foam)
4 pieces of 12" × 6" × 1" Rigid Extruded Polystyrene Foam (commonly known as pink or blue insulation foam)
Titebond® Wood Glue
Rosco® FlexBond
Castin'Craft® Mold Builder Liquid Latex Rubber or Kangaroo® Liquid Latex
Valspar® Medallion® Interior Acrylic Paint (Touch of Tan) or Rosco® Supersaturated™ Scenic Paints: White, Raw Sienna, Earth Umber

Design Master® Glossy Wood Tone Spray
FEV (French Enamel Varnish):
    Bulls Eye® Amber Shellac
    Brown Leather Dye
    Denatured Alcohol
Minwax® Wood Finish™ Stain, English Chestnut
Rosco® Premiere Clear Water Based Polyurethane Gloss

Tools

- Japanese Ryoba Saw
- Band Saw
- Stanley® Surform® Shaver™ or Pocket Plane™ or Sandpaper
- Finish Nails

Cut 5 pieces of 1" rigid extruded polystyrene foam 12" × 18". Apply a uniform coat of Titebond® Wood Glue to each piece of foam. Stack one layer on top of the next. Make sure the glue is touching the entire surface of each layer. Place a heavy object on the stack of five layers of foam to prevent sliding and air pockets between layers while the glue is drying. Allow the glue to cure for at least 24–36 hours.

Figure 30.2: Foam shaped in the form of a turkey breast

Figure 30.1: Laminating foam with wood glue

Cut the foam to resemble a turkey breast using a band saw and/or Japanese Ryoba saw. It should have a slightly elliptical and domed shape. Shape the edges using a Stanley® Surform® Shaver™. Once the general shape is created, an orbital or palm sander can be used to smooth out the overall shape of the foam.

turkey 159

Figure 30.3: Foam being shaped for legs and wings

Figure 30.4: Close-up of wing

Figure 30.5: Trough on backside of wing

Laminate 4 pieces of 1" rigid extruded polystyrene foam 6" × 12". Apply a uniform coat of Titebond® Wood Glue to each piece of foam. Stack one layer on top of another layer to create two pieces of foam 6" × 12" and 2" thick. Make sure the glue is touching the entire surface of each layer. Place a heavy object on the assembled five layers of foam to prevent sliding and air pockets between layers while the glue is drying. Allow the glue to cure for at least 24–36 hours.

Find a template online or freehand cartoon turkey legs and wings on to the foam. Cut the shapes out using the band saw. Shape the edges using a Stanley® Surform® Shaver™ to reflect the research image.

Carve a trough on the back of each of the wings so they will seat against the body of the turkey.

Use Titebond® Wood Glue or Rosco® FlexBond to attach the legs and wings to the body of the turkey. Pin the legs and wings to the body with finish nails to help them stay in place while the adhesive cures.

After the adhesive dries, remove finish nails and use a Stanley® Surform® Shaver™ to reshape the legs and wings to fit closer to the body and blend into the body, not sticking out from it.

Figure 30.6: Legs and wings attached to body of turkey

160 main entrées and side dishes

Figure 30.7: A bit of fine-tuning was done to the legs and wings after it was papier-mâchéd with brown paper towels on foam

Figure 30.8: Turkey coated in liquid latex

Figure 30.9: Turkey with sawdust texture skin and coated in FEV

Tear brown paper towels into irregular shapes. Be sure to get rid of any factory edge. The paper towels will create the skin of the turkey, the skin web between the legs, wings, and the body, and it will also smooth out the shape of the foam. Papier-mâché the paper towels on to the foam with a diluted mixture of Rosco® FlexBond and water (2:1). Adding the paper to the foam can create any modifications needed to make the foam resemble the research by accentuating peaks and blending the pieces of foam together. *Note: Fig. 30.7 shows the turkey with newly reshaped legs and wings. The modified wings and legs were not papier-mâchéd with brown paper towels to expedite the process.*

After the papier-mâché is dry, apply two layers of liquid latex. The layers of latex will replicate the skin on the turkey. It takes about 5–10 minutes for the surface to dry to do an additional coat. Liquid latex takes about an hour to totally dry.

Once the latex has dried, paint the entire body with acrylic paint to create a uniform basecoat. Valspar® Medallion® Touch of Tan Acrylic Paint was used, but mixing Rosco® Off Broadway™ White, Raw Sienna, and Earth Umber would yield a similar result. While the paint is still wet, sprinkle sawdust all over the turkey.

Coat the turkey in FEV and Minwax® English Chestnut Wood Finish™ Stain. FEV stands for French enamel varnish. FEV was originally used in cabinet making for traditional French polishing. It is a completely transparent glaze with a great depth of color. Not only is it transparent, but also it is durable, will seep into crevices and details, and it dries very quickly. To make FEV, mix 1 part shellac to 10 parts denatured alcohol. Add leather dye to reach the desired color. You can use either clear or amber shellac. It won't affect the color of the FEV. Let dry completely for 15–30 minutes.

turkey **161**

In a well-ventilated area or under a spray hood, lightly spray with Design Master® Glossy Wood Tone to add a browning variation to the skin that would occur in the roasting process. Seal with Rosco® Premiere Clear Water Based Polyurethane Gloss.

On the companion website, there is a recipe for a roasted goose that could be used to create the large Christmas goose required for productions of Charles Dickens's *A Christmas Carol*.

Figure 30.10: Close-up of applying polyurethane to turkey

Section 5
beverages

thirty one
beer

Total Time: 2 hours

Why This Works—When you heat the Gel Wax® to a higher temperature, it will produce more bubbles as the wax cools. Heating it to a temperature near 215°F will produce numerous bubbles when poured.

The gel candle wax is tintable and durable, and has a realistic weight for the end product. It is a low-density candle wax that is long lasting and odorless. Adding a dash of color from the Yaley™ concentrated candle dye to the wax tints the entire wax. All of Yaley's candle dyes are compatible with the gel wax. If the budget is an issue, there has been success in tinting the wax by using crayons.

Smooth-On® FlexFoam-iT!® V is a two-part urethane foam that expands 11 times its initial volume and cures quickly. Mix equal parts by volume. It has a pot life of 50 seconds and cures in 2 hours.

Ingredients

Yaley™ Gel Wax®
Yaley™ Gold Concentrated Candle Dye
Bulls Eye® Clear Shellac or Rosco® Premiere Clear Water Based Polyurethane Gloss
Smooth-On® FlexFoam-iT!® V (less than a tablespoon)

Tools

- Saucepan
- Candle Thermometer
- 8 oz. Plastic Mixing Cups
- Beer Mug

Safety Precautions

- Always read and follow manufacturers' instructions.
- Wear safety glasses, long sleeves, and gloves when working with Smooth-On® products.
    - Use in a well-ventilated area and avoid directly inhaling mixing agents.
- Don't pour any wax down the drain.
- Never leave melting wax unattended.
- Use a thermometer to monitor the temperature of the wax.
    - Don't overheat the wax. It will melt around 130°F. The optimum temperature for this recipe is 215°F. Heat to a maximum of 220°F.
- Keep the wax away from an open flame.
- Always use a potholder when handling a hot pot.
- Always keep an ABC fire extinguisher nearby.
- Always read and follow all manufacturers' instructions.

Figure 31.1: Gel Wax® melting in saucepan

Melt a 6″ × 6″ block of Gel Wax® in a saucepan on low heat. When the wax is melted, add gold concentrated dye shavings to reach the desired color of the beer. Using a candle thermometer heat the wax until it is close to 215°F, then pour into glass.

After pouring Gel Wax® into beer mug, allow it to completely cool and set. Once the wax is set, seal it with a coat of clear shellac. This is an important step. If the gel wax isn't sealed, the colorants in the Gel Wax® will leach into the foam. An alternative to sealing the Gel Wax® with shellac would be sealing it with Rosco® Premiere Clear.

Smooth-On® FlexFoam-iT!® V is a two-part urethane foam. Mix the parts by volume (1A:1B). Since we only needed a small amount, we used 8 oz. clear plastic cups so we could use the ridges of the cup as a measurement tool. The website suggests thoroughly pre-mixing (stir or shake) Part A and Part B separately before dispensing. For best results, the manufacturer recommends pre-mixing Part B with a mechanical mixer or drill before adding Part A *into* Part B.

For this project, a small amount of Part A was poured into the clear plastic cup halfway to the bottom ridge. Then pour Part B into the cup until it reaches the top of the ridge.

Once you add the two parts together, mix quickly and deliberately for a minimum of 15 seconds before pouring. Don't forget to aggressively scrape the sides and bottom several times when you are mixing the parts together. Pour into mold carefully. Don't splash the liquid out of the container. Don't delay between mixing and pouring. These materials cure very quickly. The pot life for this foam is 50 seconds and it will be completely set in 2 hours.

Pour on top of the beer-colored Gel Wax® that has been sealed. Let it sit for 2 hours to cure completely.

Figure 31.2: Colored Gel Wax® in beer mug

Figure 31.3: FlexFoam-iT!® V being mixed

thirty two
hot chocolate

hot chocolate

Total Time: 1 hour

Why This Works—The gel candle wax is tintable and durable, and has a realistic weight for the end product. It is a low-density candle wax that is long lasting and odorless. Adding a dash of color from the Yaley™ concentrated candle dye to the wax tints the entire wax. All of Yaley's candle dyes are compatible with the gel wax. If the budget is an issue, there has been success in tinting the wax by using crayons.

Crayola® Model Magic® is a modeling compound that is non-toxic and easily manipulated. It is remarkably lightweight, clean, resilient, and non-crumbling. It is available in a wide variety of colors and dries in 24–36 hours.

Safety Precautions

- Don't pour any wax down the drain.
- Never leave melting wax unattended.
- Use a thermometer to monitor the temperature of the wax.
  - Don't overheat the wax. It will melt around 130°F. The optimum temperature is between 160°F and 170°F. Heat to a maximum of 220°F.
- Keep the wax away from an open flame.
- Always use a potholder when handling a hot pot.
- Always keep an ABC fire extinguisher nearby.
- Always read and follow all manufacturers' instructions.

Ingredients

Yaley™ Gel Wax®
Yaley™ Brown Concentrated Candle Dye
Yaley™ White Concentrated Candle Dye
Crayola® Model Magic®, white

Tools

- 3 oz. Bathroom Dixie® Cups
- Craft Stick or Spoon
- Saucepan
- Irish Coffee Mug

Melt a 4" × 4" block of Gel Wax® in a saucepan on low heat to create the hot chocolate. The exact size of wax needed may vary based on the glassware used. When the wax is melted, add brown and white concentrated candle dye shavings to reach the desired color of the hot chocolate.

Crayola® Model Magic® is used to make the mini marshmallows. Tear off small pieces of the modeling compound. Roll into small balls and flatten on two sides.

Pour the colored molten wax into the Irish coffee mug. Add the marshmallows so some will be submerged in the wax and some will be on top of the hot chocolate. Set aside to cool.

170 beverages

Figure 32.1: Melted Gel Wax® with colorant in saucepan

Figure 32.2: Crayola® Model Magic® shaped in the form of mini marshmallows

thirty three
irish coffee

172 beverages

Total Time: 3 hours

Why This Works—The gel candle wax is tintable and durable, and has a realistic weight for the end product. It is a low-density candle wax that is long lasting and odorless. Adding a dash of color from the Yaley™ concentrated candle dye to the wax tints the entire wax. All of Yaley's candle dyes are compatible with the gel wax. If the budget is an issue, there has been success in tinting the wax by using crayons.

Smooth-On® FlexFoam-iT!® III expands 15 times its initial volume. It rises and cures quickly to a solid flexible foam. Mix ratio is 1:2 Part A to Part B. FlexFoam-iT!® III is the lowest density foam and expands the most. It has a pot life of 35 seconds and cures in 2 hours.

Safety Precautions

- Wear safety glasses, long sleeves, and gloves when working with Smooth-On® products.
  - Use in a well-ventilated area and avoid directly inhaling mixing agents.
- Don't pour any wax down the drain.
- Never leave melting wax unattended.
- Use a thermometer to monitor the temperature of the wax.
  - Don't overheat the wax. It will melt around 130°F. The optimum temperature is between 160°F and 170°F. Heat to a maximum of 220°F.
- Keep the wax away from an open flame.
- Always use a potholder when handling a hot pot.
- Always keep an ABC fire extinguisher nearby.
- Always read and follow all manufacturers' instructions.

Ingredients

Yaley™ Gel Wax®
Yaley™ Brown Concentrated Candle Dye
Smooth-On® FlexFoam-iT!® III
Bulls Eye® Clear Shellac

Tools

- 3 oz. Bathroom Dixie® Cups
- Craft Stick or Spoon
- Saucepan
- Irish Coffee Mug

Figure 33.1: Melted Gel Wax® with colorant in saucepan

Melt a 4" × 4" block of Gel Wax® in a saucepan on low heat to create the coffee. The exact size of wax needed may vary based on the glassware used. When the wax is melted, add half of a block of brown concentrated dye to reach the desired color of the coffee.

Pour the colored molten wax into the Irish coffee mug. Set aside to cool. *Caution: the glass will be very hot after pouring the wax, so be extremely careful if you need to move the glass before the wax has cooled.*

Once the gel wax is cooled, seal the top of surface of the coffee with Bulls Eye® Clear Shellac. Next, the whipped cream can be made. The cream is made by using Smooth-On® FlexFoam-iT!® III. It is a two-part urethane foam. The parts are determined by volume. Measure 1 part Part A and 2 parts Part B into separate plastic containers. Since we only needed a small amount, we used 3 oz. Dixie® Bathroom Cups. The website suggests pre-mixing Part B with a mechanical mixer or drill before adding Part A *into* Part B. Mix for 30 seconds before pouring. Make sure you stir thoroughly and scrape the sides and bottom of the cup. You need to work quickly; the pot life is about 35 seconds.

Use a craft stick to mix the two parts together. Plop the foam on top of the wax. The foam will be tacky to the touch after 30 minutes and it will be completely set in 2 hours.

Figure 33.2: 3 oz. Bathroom Dixie® Cups with FlexFoam-iT!® III

Figure 33.3: Completed Irish coffee

thirty four
lemonade

Total Time: 1 hour 30 minutes to make, 24 hours until fully set

Why This Works—Smooth-On® Encapso® K is a water clear encapsulation rubber. It is a two-part liquid mixed together in equal parts. It cures to a soft rubber texture. Without any colorant, it is clear as water. It lasts a long time. After it is cured, you can shave the Encapso® K to look like broken glass, diamonds, or ice. You can add color to it with Silc Pig® or Ignite® color pigments from Smooth-On®. Encapso® K can be removed by cutting or crumbling it away. If you want to remove it from a glass object, simply coat the glass object in petroleum jelly or Ease Release® 200 before pouring the Encapso® K.

Buying the trial-size kits is an economical way to do projects.

Purchasing plastic lemon slices and acrylic ice cubes is a time saver. You can augment the commercially produced product to make it look more realistic. Often, the items you purchase look fake because the finish isn't right. Whether the finish is too glossy, too dull, too vibrant, or the wrong color, or the texture is too smooth or too rough, taking the time to modify it will create a more aesthetically pleasing end result. For this project, Liquitex® String Gel was used to enhance the texture of the yellow flesh of the plastic lemon slice. The slice had flat finish and flat texture. Liquitex® String Gel or Golden® Clear Tar Gel are clear mediums designed to create Jackson Pollock-style drippy, stringy painting. They are available at most art supply stores like Michael's. Rosco® CrystalGel or Sculpt or Coat® could be used to achieve the same effect.

Show Application—This recipe could be used as set dressing on the porch in *Picnic* by William Inge.

Safety Precautions

- Always read and follow manufacturers' instructions.
- Use Encapso® K in a properly ventilated area.
  - Wear safety glasses, long sleeves, and vinyl gloves.
  - Latex gloves will inhibit its curing.
  - Don't apply this product to the skin.
  - Pre-mix Part A by shaking the container vigorously before measuring it for your project. Don't shake the Part B container. Shaking may create air bubbles.

Ingredients

Smooth-On® Encapso® K (1½ trial kits used in this project)
Smooth-On® Ignite® Fluorescent Pink Concentrated Pigment for Silicone
Liquitex® String Gel
Plastic Lemon Slices
Acrylic Ice Cubes

Tools

- 32 oz. or larger Plastic Mixing Cup
- Medicine Dropper
- Pitcher and Glasses for Lemonade

Figure 34.1: Pink-tinted Encapso®K in a mixing cup

Before dispensing the Part A liquid into the mixing cup, either shake or stir vigorously the material in the packaged container. Don't shake Part B.

From the first trial kit, empty parts Part A and Part B into the mixing cup. With a medicine dropper, add one drop of Ignite® Pink Concentrated Pigment. Stir thoroughly, scraping the sides and bottom to make sure all the pigment is incorporated. You have a 2-hour pot life for this product.

Pour first batch into glass pitcher, which will fill it up about halfway. Wait 90 minutes for the Encapso®K to begin to cure. Place acrylic ice cubes in the lemonade. Make a second batch of the Encapso® K pink lemonade to finish filling the pitcher and glass. You only need to wait about 10 minutes after placing the acrylic ice cubes before pouring the rest of the lemonade into the pitcher. Don't move the pitcher for 24 hours until it fully cures. Do the same for the glass.

Commercially produced plastic lemon slices were purchased. A matte knife was used to cut a notch in the slice so it can sit on the side of the glass or pitcher. Liquitex® String Gel can be used to enhance the texture of the endocarp (yellow flesh) of the lemon. Place a slice on the rim of the glass and on the rim of the pitcher.

Figure 34.2: Pitcher partially filled with Encapso® K before adding acrylic ice cubes

Figure 34.3: Plastic lemon with added embellishments

thirty five

martini with olives

Total Time: 45 minutes to make, 24 hours until fully set

Why This Works—Smooth-On® Encapso® K is a water clear encapsulation rubber. It is a two-part liquid mixed together in equal parts. It cures to a soft rubber texture. Without any colorant, it is clear as water. It lasts a long time. After it is cured, you can shave the Encapso® K to look like broken glass, diamonds, or ice. You can add color to it with Silc Pig® or Ignite® color pigments from Smooth-On®. Encapso® K can be removed by cutting or crumbling it away. If you want to remove it from a glass object, simply coat the glass object in petroleum jelly or Ease Release® 200 before pouring the Encapso® K.

Buying the trial-size kits is an economical way to do projects. Another slightly less expensive option for a hardened translucent liquid is also available on Amazon.com and Walmart.com called FloralCraft® Acrylic Water Kit. It is a two-part, clear, hard-setting gel. The kit comes with 4 oz. of resin, 4 oz. of hardener, a disposable tray, and a stick for mixing. It sets in 24–48 hours.

Scenic paint was used to paint the olives, but any acrylic paint can be used. A nice substitution is PLAID® FolkArt® Acrylic Paint in Yellow Citron. The FolkArt® acrylic paint is a premium, all-purpose paint. It is certified AP non-toxic, water based, and acid neutral.

Safety Precautions

- Always read and follow manufacturers' instructions.
- Use Encapso® K in a properly ventilated area.
  - Wear safety glasses, long sleeves, and vinyl gloves.
  - Latex gloves will inhibit its curing.
  - Don't apply this product to the skin.
  - Pre-mix Part A by shaking the container vigorously before measuring it for your project. Don't shake the Part B container as it may create air bubbles.

Ingredients

Smooth-On® Encapso® K (trial kit used in this project)
Crayola® Model Magic®, white
Rosco® Super Saturated™ Scenic Paints: Ultramarine Blue, Yellow Ochre, Bright Chrome Oxide Green.
Rosco® Premiere Clear Water Based Polyurethane Gloss or Rosco® Clear Acrylic Gloss

Tools

- Two 8 oz. Clear Plastic Mixing Cups
- Stirring Stick
- Paint Brush
- Toothpick
- Martini Glass

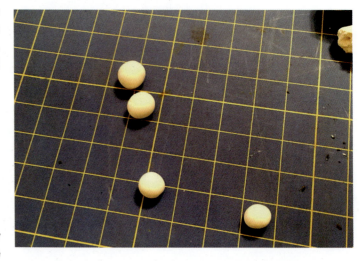

Figure 35.1: Crayola® Model Magic® shaped into balls for olives

Create the olives first so that they can be submerged in the liquid. Using Crayola® Model Magic®, roll two balls about the size of a penny. The shape and size of the olives can be different depending on the research, the size of the martini glass, and the distance from the stage prop to the audience. Let air-dry for 30 minutes on toothpick before painting.

To paint the olives, mix Rosco® Super Saturated™ Ultramarine Blue, Yellow Ochre, and a touch of Chrome Oxide Green to create the green olive color. Adding a small dab of a red paint can represent the stuffed pimento. Seal the olives with Rosco® Premiere Clear Water Based Polyurethane Gloss or Rosco® Clear Acrylic Gloss after the paint has dried. If the paint isn't sealed, it may hinder the curing rate or stop the Encapso® K from curing all together. When the sealer is dry,

Figure 35.3: Painted olives drying

firmly attach the toothpick with the olives to the glass before pouring the liquid component. If the toothpick with olives isn't secured, it will float to the top of the glass while the Encapso® K cures.

Figure 35.2: Unpainted olives in glass

Figure 35.4: Two parts of Encapso® K in clear plastic cups

Encapso® K is used for the liquid part of the martini. Before dispensing the Part A liquid into the mixing cup, either shake or stir vigorously the material in the packaged container. Don't shake Part B.

Empty parts Part A and Part B into separate mixing cups. Clear plastic cups are helpful so you can see the exact amounts of each part before pouring them together. Combine into one container. Stir thoroughly, scraping the sides and bottom to make sure both parts are incorporated well. You have a 2-hour pot life for this product.

Make sure the toothpick with olives is secured to the glass in the desired position. Pour the mixed Encapso® K into the martini glass. Don't move the glass for 24 hours until it fully cures.

Figure 35.5: Mixing Encapso® K

Figure 35.6: Pouring Encapso® K into the martini glass

thirty six

milk

white and chocolate

Total Time: 10 minutes to make, 24 hours until fully set

Why This Works—Smooth-On® Encapso® K is a water clear encapsulation rubber. It is a two-part liquid mixed together in equal parts. It cures to a soft rubber texture. Without any colorant, it is clear as water and lasts a long time. After it is cured, you can shave the Encapso® K to look like broken glass, diamonds, or ice. You can add color to it with Silc Pig® or Ignite® color pigments from Smooth-On®. Encapso® K can be removed by cutting or crumbling it away. If you want to remove it from a glass object, simply coat the glass object in petroleum jelly or Ease Release® 200 before pouring the Encapso® K.

Show Application—This recipe could be used for any diner show like *Bus Stop* by William Inge or *Spitfire Grill* by James Valcq and Fred Alley, or a show with breakfast like *Hay Fever* by Noël Coward.

Safety Precautions

- Always read and follow manufacturers' instructions.
- Use Encapso® K in a properly ventilated area.
  - Wear safety glasses, long sleeves, and vinyl gloves.
  - Latex gloves will inhibit its curing.
  - Don't apply this product to the skin.
  - Pre-mix Part A by shaking the container vigorously before measuring it for your project. Don't shake the Part B container as shaking may create air bubbles.

Ingredients

Smooth-On® Encapso® K
Smooth-On® Silc Pig® White Concentrated Pigment for Silicone
Smooth-On® Silc Pig® Brown Concentrated Pigment for Silicone

Tools

- 8 oz. Plastic Mixing Cups
- Medicine Dropper
- Glasses for milk

Before dispensing the Part A liquid into the mixing cup, either shake or stir vigorously the material in the packaged container. Don't shake Part B. Pour equal parts Part A and Part B into the mixing cup leaving a little room to stir the two together. With a medicine dropper, add two drops of Silc Pig® White Concentrated Pigment. Stir thoroughly, scraping the sides and bottom to make sure all the pigment is incorporated. You have a 2-hour pot life for this product. Pour into glass. Don't move the glass for 24 hours until it fully cures.

Figure 36.1: Completed white milk   Figure 36.2: Completed chocolate milk

Before dispensing the Part A liquid into the mixing cup, either shake or stir vigorously the material in the packaged container. Don't shake Part B. Pour equal parts Part A and Part B into the mixing cup leaving a little room to stir the two together. With a medicine dropper, add one drop of Silc Pig® White and half a drop of Brown Concentrated Pigment until it becomes the desired chocolate milk color. Stir thoroughly, scraping the sides and bottom to make sure all the pigment is incorporated. You have a 2-hour pot life for this product. Pour into glass. Don't move the glass for 24 hours until it fully cures.

The same technique can be applied to create orange juice by using a combination of Silc Pig® red, yellow, and white.

Figure 36.3: Completed orange juice

thirty seven

piña colada

piña colada 185

Total Time: 2 hours prep, 24 hours to cure

Why This Works—Smooth-On® Encapso® K is a water clear encapsulation rubber. It is a two-part liquid mixed together in equal parts. It cures to a soft rubber texture. It has a 2-hour pot life and takes 24 hours to cure. Without any colorant, it is clear as water. It lasts a long time. It is also UV-resistant and easy to color. After it is cured, you can shave the Encapso® K to look like broken glass, diamonds, or ice. You can add color to it with Silc Pig® or Ignite® color pigments from Smooth-On®. Encapso® K can be removed by cutting or crumbling it away. If you want to remove it from a glass object, simply coat the glass object in petroleum jelly or Ease Release® 200 before pouring the Encapso® K.

Smooth-On® FlexFoam-iT!® V is a two-part urethane foam that expands 11 times its initial volume and cures quickly. Mix equal parts by volume. It has a pot life of 50 seconds and cures in 2 hours.

Ingredients

Smooth-On® Encapso® K
Smooth-On® Silc Pig® White Concentrated Pigment for Silicone
Wood Shavings
Fake Cherries
Smooth-On® FlexFoam-iT!® V
Design Master® Glossy Wood Tone Spray

Tools

- 16 oz. Plastic Mixing Cup
- Medicine Dropper
- Plastic Sandwich Bag
- Piña Colada Glass also known as a Poco Grande Glass

Safety Precautions

- Always read and follow all manufacturers' instructions.
- Wear safety glasses, long sleeves, and gloves when working with Smooth-On® products.
  - Use in a well-ventilated area and avoid directly inhaling mixing agents.
- Use Encapso® K in a properly ventilated area.
  - Wear safety glasses, long sleeves, and vinyl gloves.
  - Latex gloves will inhibit its curing.
  - Don't apply this product to the skin.
  - Pre-mix Part A by shaking the container vigorously before measuring it for your project. Don't shake the Part B container as shaking may create air bubbles.

Figure 37.1: Encapso® K

186 beverages

Before dispensing the Part A liquid into the mixing cup, either shake or stir vigorously the material in the packaged container. Don't shake Part B. Pour equal parts Part A and Part B into the mixing cup leaving a little room to stir the two together. With a medicine dropper, add two drops of Silc Pig® White Concentrated Pigment. Stir thoroughly, scraping the sides and bottom to make sure all the pigment is incorporated. You have a 2-hour pot life for this product.

In a plastic sandwich bag, break up the wood shavings to make smaller pieces to resemble coconut. Empty the bag of wood shavings into the Encapso® K mixture. Mix thoroughly with a spoon, scraping the sides and bottom to get all the pigment and wood shavings incorporated.

Figure 37.3: Top view of piña colada with FlexFoam-iT!® V

Figure 37.2: Encapso®K, Silc Pig®, and sawdust mixture

Pour into a piña colada glass. Don't move the glass for 24 hours until it fully cures. In a well-ventilated area, spray artificial cherries with Design Master® Glossy Wood Tone for a more realistic looking cherry.

The frothy top is created by using Smooth-On® FlexFoam-iT!® V. It is a two-part urethane foam. Mix the parts by volume. Since we only needed a small amount, we used 8 oz. clear plastic cups so we could use the ridges of the cup as a measurement tool. The website suggests thoroughly pre-mixing (stir or shake) Part A and Part B separately before dispensing. For best results, the manufacturer recommends pre-mixing Part B with a mechanical mixer or drill before adding Part A *into* Part B.

For this project, a small amount of Part A was poured into the clear plastic cup to reach an eighth of the volume of the cup. Then Part B was poured into the cup until it reached one quarter of the cup.

Once you add the two parts together, mix quickly and deliberately for a minimum of 15 seconds before pouring. Don't forget to aggressively scrape the sides and bottom several times when you are mixing the parts together. Pour into mold carefully. Don't splash the liquid out of the container. Don't delay between mixing and pouring. These materials cure very quickly. The pot life for this foam is 50 seconds and it will be completely set in 2 hours.

Pour on top of the tinted Encapso®K in the glass. Remember the foam will expand 11 times its initial volume, so leave room in the glass for the foam to expand. Add fake cherries to garnish the drink. It is helpful to rest the cherries against the edge of the glass. Let it sit for 2 hours to cure completely.

Section 6
desserts

thirty eight

apple tart

Prep/Cooking Time: 90 minutes
Total Time: 12–18 hours

Why This Works—The traditional salt dough recipe has less salt and no vegetable oil or alum. The vegetable oil and alum help to keep the dough from cracking while rolling it into shape. This salt dough recipe uses one less cup of salt. The dough remains more flexible and stays soft longer while kneading. Heating the ingredients on the stove makes the dough less sticky when rolling it out. It is important to note that this crust is baked for a longer time at lower temperature than other salt dough recipes in this book. When the salt dough is baked at a higher temperature like 350°F, the dough puffs up more. By baking this crust at 200°F for an hour, the dough doesn't bubble up.

Insulation (extruded polystyrene) foam is quite easy to form and cut. It comes in a variety of thicknesses. Buying the contractor pack of ½ thick foam is cost-effective. It can be laminated together with either 3M™ Fastbond™ 30NF Contact Adhesive or Elmer's® Glue-All®. For this recipe, Elmer's® Glue-All® was used. The benefit is this is slightly less expensive and readily available. A lot of glue is needed to laminate the sheets of foam and it needs to be clamped well while it dries. It typically comes in two colors, pink and blue. The pink extruded polystyrene (XPS) is produced by Owens Corning® Foamular® and the blue XPS is produced by Dow™ Styrofoam™.

The gel candle wax is tintable and durable, and has a realistic weight for the end product. It is a low-density candle wax and is both long lasting and odorless. It can be colored by adding a dash of color from the Yaley™ concentrated candle dye to the wax. It tints the entire wax. All of Yaley's candle dyes are compatible with the gel wax. If the budget is an issue, there has been success in tinting the wax by using crayons.

Safety Precautions

- Don't pour any wax down the drain.
- Never leave melting wax unattended.
- Use a thermometer to monitor the temperature of the wax.
  - Don't overheat the wax. It will melt around 130°F. The optimum temperature is between 160°F and 170°F. Heat to a maximum of 220°F.
- Keep the wax away from an open flame.
- Always use a potholder when handling a hot pot.
- Always keep an ABC fire extinguisher nearby.
- Always read and follow all manufacturers' instructions.

Ingredients

Pie Crust
Salt Dough:
  2 c. Flour
  1 c. Salt
  1 c. Water
  2 tbsp. Vegetable Oil
  2 tbsp. Alum
PAM® Cooking Spray

Apple Filling
½" Extruded Polystyrene Insulation Foam (pink or blue foam)
Crayola® Model Magic®, white
Rosco® Off Broadway™ Scenic Paint:
Bulls Eye® Amber Shellac
Elmer's® Glue-All®
Design Master® Glossy Wood Tone Spray

Caramel Drizzle
Yaley™ Gel Wax®
Yaley™ Yellow Concentrated Candle Dye or Yellow Crayon
Yaley™ Brown Concentrated Candle Dye or Brown Crayon

Tools

- 9" Fluted Tart Pan
- Saucepan
- Spoon
- Rolling Pin
- Ruler
- 2" Crescent Moon Cookie Cutter

smooth and thick. Make a ball. Use immediately or refrigerate in an airtight container. Using a rolling pin, roll dough out so it is less than 1/8" thick and roughly a 14" diameter circle. Place the dough in tart plate, pressing it into the bottom and sides. Bake at 200°F for 60 minutes. The dough will puff up less if it is baked at a lower temperature. When the crust turns white and dry, take it out of the oven. Let cool.

Figure 38.2: Dough in 9" tart pan in oven

Figure 38.1: Tart pan sprayed with PAM® and lightly floured

Preheat oven to 200°F. Spray the tart pan with PAM® Cooking Spray and lightly flour. To make the salt dough, mix the dry ingredients in a saucepan. Add water and vegetable oil. Heat over low heat until it is the consistency of mashed potatoes, stirring until there are no more clumps. Using a plastic spoon, scoop it out on to a lightly floured surface. Knead it until it is

While crust is cooling, cut a round disk of pink insulation foam for the base of the filling in the tart. A 9" cake pan can be used for a template to draw this circle.

Apple Slices

Roll out Model Magic® until it is about 1/8" thick. Use a 2" crescent moon cookie cutter to make apple slices. Vary the shapes by modifying the edges a little to resemble the organic nature of apples. Let the apple slices air-dry overnight to harden.

192 desserts

Figure 38.3: Baked crust cooling

Figure 38.4: 9" disk of XPS foam being primed for base of tart filling

Figure 38.5: Cutting apple slices out of Crayola® Model Magic®

Figure 38.6: Apple slices air-drying to harden

Figure 38.7: Assembled tart

Once the crust has cooled, coat it with amber shellac to give it a golden brown color. Let it dry and flip the crust out of the tin. Turn the tart pan upside down on a cookie sheet and place the crust on the outside of the pan so the dough will hold its shape. Put it back in the oven to thoroughly cook the bottom for 5 to 10 minutes. If you have time, you can let the bottom of the crust air-dry rather than putting it back in the oven. Once the crust has cooled again, coat the bottom with amber shellac. Be sure to add a little more shellac to areas that would have browned more in the baking process. Coating with amber shellac will both preserve the dough and add browning details to the crust.

Once shellac has dried, place a primed XPS foam base into crust and glue. Glue apple slices to base. Paint to look like apple slices by adding a layer of Rosco yellow ochre mixed with white and a little earth umber. When paint is dry, add a layer of amber shellac to the edges and areas of the slices that may have browned more in the oven. Add a few spritzes of Design Master® Glossy Wood Tone Spray to the tart to add more toning.

Caramel Drizzle

Melt two 2″ × 2″ blocks of Gel Wax® into a saucepan on medium heat. Create $1/16$″ shavings of yellow and brown colorant or crayons to tint the Gel Wax®. Add 4 shavings of yellow and 2 shavings of brown to the Gel Wax®. Stir thoroughly. Check the color and add more colorant until desired color is reached. Drizzle over the apple slices in pie shell. Caramel drizzle can puddle in select places in the pie and a few dribbles can be on the crust. Cool completely before moving.

Figure 38.8: Painted apples in pie tart

Figure 38.10: Completed tart

Figure 38.9: Melting Gel Wax® with colorant in saucepan for caramel drizzle

thirty nine

cake with removable piece

Total Time: 2 hours 30 minutes of prep, 48 hours to dry

Why This Works—Often shows call for only a small portion of cake to be eaten on stage. The tricky part is figuring out a way to create a fake prop with non-toxic or food-safe components with an edible portion inset. Using a barrier of plastic wrap, like Saran™ Wrap, between the inedible and edible portion is a must.

Insulation (extruded polystyrene) foam is quite easy to form and cut. It comes in a variety of thicknesses. It does come in contractor packs of ½" thick foam, but for this project getting the 1" foam will produce a better result. It typically comes in two colors, pink and blue. The pink extruded polystyrene (XPS) is produced by Owens Corning® Foamular® and the blue XPS is produced by Dow™ Styrofoam™. If the foam is going to be handled a lot, you may want to make sure the paint adheres well to the foam by coating the foam first with either Rosco® FoamCoat, CrystalGel, or 3M™ Fastbond™ Contact Adhesive 30NF before painting. Each of these products bonds better with the foam and helps the paint not flake off.

There are a few options for laminating the extruded polystyrene. Rosco™ FlexBond, Elmer's® Glue, Titebond® Wood Glue, and 3M® Super 77™ Classic or 78™ Spray Adhesive will all work. It is important to note that 3M™ changed the formula for Super 77™ and it now has acetone in it. Acetone will "eat" the polystyrene foam. The classic formula doesn't "eat" the foam. 3M™ has developed Polystyrene Insulation 78™ Spray Adhesive that can safely be used to adhere polystyrene foam together. Both of these spray adhesives create a stronger bond if you spray both surfaces to be laminated together and let them tack up for a minimum of 30 seconds before bonding the two surfaces together. After using any aerosol adhesive (or paint), invert the can and depress the spray tip until the spray is free of adhesive (or paint). By adopting this practice, the spray tip will not clog as frequently.

If Rosco® FlexBond, Elmer's® Glue-All®, or Titebond® Wood Glue are used, after the layers are laminated, make sure you apply enough weight on the pieces while they are drying. Using a ratchet strap will apply a substantial amount of pressure, but make sure the edges are protected from the straps cutting into the foam by placing wood blocks under the straps.

According to the product information, the benefit of using Rosco® FlexBond is it provides a flexible adhesive bond between many scenic materials, such as fabrics, plastics, foams, and wood. It dries to a clear, hard, yet pliable coating that does not suffer from the "tackiness" common in many other flexible glues even after those glues have had days to dry. And unlike ordinary "white" glues that can crack and break when flexed, the adhesive bond of Rosco® FlexBond remains extremely pliable and strong even as the materials bend and deform. It also is water based with minimal odor and fumes.

Safety Precautions

- Always read and follow all manufacturers' directions.
- Always double-check the SDS (Safety Data Sheets) for each product used and make sure the components of the product are not harmful. Companies often change the chemical makeup of their products over the years; don't assume that by checking once that the product is safe, it will always be safe.

Show Application—This recipe could be used for *Crimes of the Heart* by Beth Henley. This cake is the size of a ¼ sheet cake. Adjust the size depending on desired cake size.

Ingredients

Cake Body
3 pieces 9" × 13" of 1" Rigid Extruded Polystyrene Insulation Foam (commonly known as pink or blue foam)
Titebond® Wood Glue
Rosco® Supersaturated™ Scenic Paints: White, Yellow Ochre
Bulls Eye® Clear or Amber Shellac

desserts

> **Icing**
> Rosco® CrystalGel
> Swans Down® Cake Flour
> Rosco® Supersaturated™ Scenic Paints: your choice of colors
>
> **Edible Cake Piece**
> Sara Lee® Frozen All Butter Pound Cake
> Duncan Hines® Creamy Home-Style Classic Vanilla Frosting

Tools

- Ruler
- Marking Device (Marker or Pencil)
- Utility Knife, Hand Saw, or Band Saw to cut foam
- Palm or Orbital Sander for shaping foam
- Paint Brushes
- Mixing Containers, Small
- Icing Spatula
- Plastic Sandwich Bag or Pastry Bag
- Additional Sandwich Bag
- Star Decorating Tip or other desired cake decorating tips
- Plastic wrap similar to Saran™ Wrap

Figure 39.1: Foam laminated and painted to be a ¼ sheet cake

Cut three rectangles (9" × 13") out of 1" extruded polystyrene insulation foam. Sand to smooth edges. This is the size of a ¼ sheet cake. Adjust the size depending on desired cake size.

Laminate the foam pieces together. For this recipe, Titebond® Wood Glue was used. Spread an ample amount of glue evenly on the surfaces of the foam. To ensure a strong bond, place weight on the pieces as they are drying.

Once the glue is dry, remove any excess foam or glue from the outer edges by using a hand saw or band saw. Use an orbital or palm sander to shape the rectangles into a realistic cake shape, easing or rounding-over the edges.

Decide where the removable piece is going to be and cut away the appropriate size foam. For this project, a corner was chosen.

Paint foam an off-white or cream color using Rosco® Supersaturated™ white, yellow ochre, and/or burnt umber to match actual cake color. If the foam is going to be handled a lot, you may want to make sure the paint adheres well to the foam by first coating the foam with either Rosco® FoamCoat, CrystalGel, or 3M™ Fastbond™ Contact Adhesive 30NF before painting. Each of those products bonds better with the foam and helps the paint not flake off as easily.

Figure 39.2: Gluing plastic wrap to inside of cut-out where edible piece will be

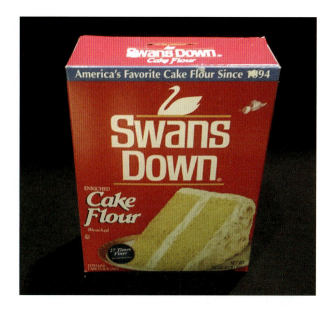

Figure 39.3A: Swans Down® cake flour added to Rosco® CrystalGel creates a texture similar to actual icing

Coat the painted foam with Bulls Eye® Shellac or another sealer. Once Bulls Eye® Shellac is dry, it is durable, all natural, non-toxic, and food-safe according to the Rockler Woodworking website. Despite the claims that it is food-safe, cover the exposed foam cake with Saran™ Wrap or other plastic food-safe wrap to form a barrier between the foam and the parts that will be eaten. Make sure you have plastic overlapping all edges that the edible items will be touching.

For the fake icing, mix equal parts Rosco® CrystalGel and Swans Down® cake flour to create the base for the icing. Adding cake flour to CrystalGel creates a texture closer to actual icing. Cake flour worked better than all-purpose flour because it is more finely ground and has less protein. In edible baked goods, it bakes into fluffy cakes. Tint the mixture with

Figure 39.3B: Mixing the fake icing

198 desserts

Figure 39.4: Icing the fake cake

Figure 39.5A: Frosting the inside edges of plastic wrap-covered foam cake to insert edible cake piece

Rosco® Supersaturated™ or Off Broadway™ paints to desired color of icing. Mix thoroughly. Adjust paint added to match your research image. For this project, vanilla frosting was chosen. Once the fake frosting is mixed, frost foam cake using an icing spatula. Create an even coat on the top and sides, ideally ¼" to ½" thick. Near the area for the portion that will be eaten, feather the fake frosting out in anticipation of blending the edible frosting to the fake frosting seamlessly. Let base layer of icing cure overnight until it is hard.

Cut a piece of the defrosted Sara Lee® All Butter Pound Cake to match the size of the missing piece. For this project, the size of the pound cake was 3" × 2¾" × 3".

To insert the edible cake piece, first, apply a thin coat of edible frosting to the plastic wrap sides of the foam cake. Inset the actual cake into the foam cake. Blend the actual

Figure 39.5B: Trimming the pound cake to fit in the fake cake

cake with removable piece 199

Figure 39.5C: Edible cake inset in the fake cake

Figure 39.6: Piping stars on cake

Figure 39.5D: Frosting edible cake insert to blend into the fake cake

frosting with the faux frosting. Depending on the gap, it may be necessary to pipe frosting into the seam. Smooth out the frosting.

Once the top icing has set, place the remainder of the icing mixture in a pastry bag or plastic sandwich bag with a star tip attached. Pipe icing stars on the top and bottom outside edge of the cake. To create stars, fold down the top of the pastry bag or plastic sandwich bag to remove the air and get the icing mixture down to the tip. Keep a hand on the folded edge, holding the bag with the star tip perpendicular to the surface, squeeze the bag to create a dollop of icing of the desired size. As you release the pressure on the bag, pull straight up so you get a nice little point like Hershey's® Kisses®. Or you can do a rope border. Wilton.com describes the technique of creating a rope border by holding the pastry bag with a star tip at a 39° angle. Use steady, even pressure, squeeze while moving the tip in a gentle sideways "S" curve. Stop pressure and pull the tip away. Then nest the start of the next "S" in the bottom curve of the previous "S" shape. Keep spacing and curves uniform in thickness, length, and overall size.

Figure 39.7: Completed cake in shop

Figure 39.8: The icing color could be changed to chocolate. Chocolate icing tends to hide the edible piece better. This image shows an alternative placement for the edible piece of cake.

forty

cherry pie

202 desserts

Total Time: 4 hours

Why This Works—The traditional salt dough recipe has less salt and no vegetable oil or alum. The vegetable oil and alum help to keep the dough from cracking while rolling it into shape. Heating the ingredients on the stove makes the dough less sticky when rolling it out. It is important to note that this crust is baked for a shorter time at lower temperature than other salt dough recipes in this book. When the salt dough is baked at a higher temperature like 350°F, the dough puffs up more. By baking this crust at 250°F for only 15 minutes, the dough doesn't puff up.

The gel candle wax is tintable and durable, and has a realistic weight for the end product. When crème wax is added to gel wax, it gives the gel wax more structure and reduces the bubbles. The wax will set faster. Both are low-density candle waxes that are long lasting and odorless. Adding a dash of color from the Yaley™ concentrated candle dye to the wax tints the entire wax. All of Yaley's candle dyes are compatible with the gel wax. If the budget is an issue, there has been success in tinting the wax by using crayons.

Show Application—This pie was built for University of Cincinnati College-Conservatory of Music's production of *Into the Woods* by Stephen Sondheim and James Lapine.

Safety Precautions

- Always read and follow all manufacturers' directions.
- Don't pour any wax down the drain.
- Never leave melting wax unattended.
- Use a thermometer to monitor the temperature of the wax.
  - Don't overheat the wax. It will melt around 130°F. The optimum temperature is between 160°F and 170°F. Heat to a maximum of 220°F.
- Keep the wax away from an open flame.
- Always use a potholder when handling a hot pot.
- Always keep an ABC fire extinguisher nearby.

Ingredients

Salt Dough
2 c. Flour
2 c. Salt
1 c. Water
2 tbsp. Vegetable Oil
2 tbsp. Alum
PAM® Cooking Spray
Yaley™ Gel Wax®
Yaley™ Crème Wax®
Yaley™ Cranberry Concentrated Candle Dye
Yaley™ Red Concentrated Candle Dye
Fake Grapes
Bulls Eye® Amber Shellac
Denatured Alcohol
Design Master® Glossy Wood Tone Spray

Tools

- 9" Pie Pan
- Saucepan
- Candle Thermometer

Preheat oven to 250°F. Spray the pie pan with PAM® Cooking Spray. To make the salt dough, mix the dry ingredients in a saucepan. Add water and vegetable oil. Heat over low heat until it is the consistency of mashed potatoes, stirring until there are no more clumps. Using a plastic spoon, scoop it out on to a lightly floured surface. Knead it until it is smooth and thick. Make a ball. Use immediately or refrigerate in an airtight container. Using a rolling pin, roll dough out so it is less than ⅛" thick. Place the dough in pie plate, pressing it into the bottom. Flute the edges by pinching the edge of the crust by pushing your thumb from one hand between the thumb and

Figure 40.1: The salt dough crust in pie pan

index finger of the opposite hand. Repeat every ½". Bake at 250°F for 15 minutes. The dough will puff up less if it is baked at a lower temperature. When the piecrust turns white and dry, take it out of the oven.

Once the crust has cooled, coat it with amber shellac to give it a golden brown color. Let it dry and flip the crust out of the tin. Turn the pie pan upside down on a cookie sheet and place the crust on the outside of the pie pan so the dough will hold its shape. Put it back in the oven to thoroughly cook the bottom for 15 minutes. Once the crust has cooled again, coat the bottom with amber shellac. Be sure to add a little more shellac to areas that would have browned more in the baking process.

Melt a 4" × 4" block of Gel Wax® or equal parts of both Gel Wax® and Crème Wax® in a saucepan on low heat to create the cherry filling. When the wax is melted, add cranberry and red concentrated dyes shavings to reach the desired color of

Figure 40.2: Baked salt dough crust coated with amber shellac

Figure 40.3: Gel Wax® with dye melting in pan

204 desserts

Figure 40.4: Pie with lattice strips

the cherry filling. Pour the colored molten wax into the piecrust. Place round plastic grapes in the Gel Wax®, submerge some of them and let some be in small groups.

While the wax is curing, place ¾" strips of salt dough on the top to create a lattice top. For a touch of additional realism, weave the strips of dough to create the lattice. Return the pie to the oven to bake the lattice top. Bake at 350°F for 15–20 minutes or until the salt dough hardens and turns white. Remove from oven and let cool. Coat the lattice and filling with a layer of diluted amber shellac. Dilute the amber shellac with denatured alcohol in the ratio of 1 part shellac to 2 parts denatured alcohol. Build up glazes of amber shellac on the crust. By diluting the amber shellac, you get the color of the amber shellac and with thinner coats the shellac doesn't build up creating an encapsulated look. Spraying Design Master® Glossy Wood Tone around the edges of the piecrust adds more definition from the baking process. Repeat coating pie in shellac until the pie is hard and can withstand the wear and tear of the show.

On the companion website, there is a bonus recipe for mini berry pies also created for *Into the Woods*.

Figure 40.5: Completed cherry pie

forty one

chocolate cake à la mode

206 desserts

Total Time: 1 hour of prep, overnight to dry

Why This Works—Insulation (extruded polystyrene) foam is quite easy to form and cut. It comes in a variety of thicknesses. It does come in contractor packs of ½" thick foam, but for this project getting the 1" foam will produce a better result. It typically comes in two colors, pink and blue. The pink extruded polystyrene (XPS) is produced by Owens Corning® Foamular® and the blue XPS is produced by Dow™ Styrofoam™. If the foam is going to be handled a lot, you may want to make sure the paint adheres well to the foam by coating the foam first with either Rosco® FoamCoat, CrystalGel, or 3M™ Fastbond™ Contact Adhesive 30NF before painting. Each of those products bonds better with the foam and helps the paint not flake off.

Using a metal ice cream scoop that has a lever and sweeper blade to form the Model Magic® creates a more realistic freshly scooped detail to the ice cream.

Safety Precautions

- Always read and follow all manufacturers' directions.

Show Application—This recipe could be used for set dressing for any diner show like *Bus Stop* by William Inge or *Spitfire Grill* by James Valcq and Fred Alley.

Ingredients

2 pieces 2" x 6" of 1" Rigid Extruded Polystyrene Insulation Foam (commonly known as pink or blue foam)

Rosco® CrystalGel

Rosco® Supersaturated™ Scenic Paints: Burnt Umber, Van Dyke Brown

Crayola® Model Magic®, white, about a tennis-ball size

Tools

- Saucepan
- Spoon
- Ruler
- Marking Device (Marker or Pencil)
- Sand Paper
- Mixing Container, Small
- Icing Spatula
- Plastic Sandwich Bag or Pastry Bag
- Additional Sandwich Bag
- Star Decorating Tip
- Ice Cream Scoop with Lever and Sweeper

Figure 41.1: Foam triangles to form wedge of cake

Cut two isosceles triangles (2" x 6") out of 1" extruded polystyrene insulation foam. Sand to smooth edges. For exceptional attention to detail, slightly curve the short edge of the triangle to mimic a wedge of cake cut from a round layer cake.

chocolate cake à la mode **207**

Figure 41.2: Foam wedges painted with burnt umber

Figure 41.3: Mixing the icing

Paint a dark chocolate brown using Rosco® Supersaturated™ Burnt Umber. If the foam is going to be handled a lot, you may want to make sure the paint adheres well to the foam by first coating the foam with either Rosco® FoamCoat, CrystalGel, or 3M™ Fastbond™ Contact Adhesive 30NF before painting. Each of those products bonds better with the foam and helps the paint not flake off as easily.

For the icing, mix 3 parts of Rosco® CrystalGel, 2 parts of Rosco® Supersaturated™ Burnt Umber and Van Dyke Brown. Mix thoroughly. Adjust paint added to match your research image. Make twice as much as you think you need.

On top of each of the wedges of foam, spoon out the icing mixture. Using an icing spatula, smooth out mixture. Let cure for 3 minutes. Carefully place one of the foam triangles on top of the other. Be gentle and do not jar the pieces because the icing in the middle hasn't fully set yet. Ice the top and back edge of the cakes with some of the remaining icing mixture.

Figure 41.4: Icing the cake

Figure 41.5: Cake with icing

Figure 41.6: Piping stars on cake

Figure 41.7: Making the scoop of ice cream

Smooth out the top and sides of the icing with the icing spatula. The decorative side scallop side of the spatula was used on the back and the flat side of the spatula was used for the top. Let dry overnight. Once fully dried, any excess icing that may have seeped out between the layers can be gently scraped off. Save the remaining icing from frosting the cake in an airtight container.

Once the top icing has set, place the remainder of the icing mixture in a pastry bag or plastic sandwich bag with a star tip attached. Place cake on final plate. Pipe icing stars on the top and bottom outside edge of the cake. To create stars, fold down the top of the pastry bag or plastic sandwich bag to remove the air and get the icing mixture down to the tip. Keeping a hand on the folded edge, hold the bag with the star tip perpendicular to the surface, squeeze the bag to create a dollop of icing of the desired size. As you release the pressure on the bag, pull straight up so you get a nice little point like Hershey's® Kisses®.

chocolate cake à la mode   **209**

Roll white Crayola® Model Magic® into a ball about the size of a tennis ball or racquet ball. Using a metal ice cream scoop with a lever and sweeper, place Model Magic® ball in scoop. Press down on a hard surface to get the clay to get the freshly scooped look of ice cream.

Use Rosco® CrystalGel to attach the ice cream to the plate with the cake.

Put about a tablespoon of icing mixture into a plastic sandwich bag. Remove most of the air from the bag and seal. Snip off a small portion of the corner of the bag. To create a chocolate drizzle over the cake and ice cream, squeeze a thin ribbon of icing from the bag.

Figure 41.8: Ice cream on top of cake

forty two

coconut cream pie

coconut cream pie

Total Time: 4 hours

Why This Works—The traditional salt dough recipe has less salt and no vegetable oil or alum. The vegetable oil and alum help to keep the dough from cracking while rolling it into shape. Heating the ingredients on the stove makes the dough less sticky when rolling it out.

The gel candle wax is tintable and durable, and has a realistic weight for the end product. It is a low-density candle wax and is long lasting and odorless. Adding a dash of color from the Yaley™ concentrated candle dye to the wax tints the entire wax. All of Yaley's candle dyes are compatible with the gel wax. If the budget is an issue, there has been success in tinting the wax by using crayons.

Safety Precautions

- Always read and follow all manufacturers' directions.
- Don't pour any wax down the drain.
- Never leave melting wax unattended.
- Use a thermometer to monitor the temperature of the wax.
  - Don't overheat the wax. It will melt around 130°F. The optimum temperature is between 160°F and 170°F. Heat to a maximum of 220°F.
- Keep the wax away from an open flame.
- Always use a potholder when handling a hot pot.
- Always keep an ABC fire extinguisher nearby.

Ingredients

Salt Dough:
- 2 c. Flour
- 2 c. Salt
- 1 c. Water
- 2 tbsp. Vegetable Oil
- 2 tbsp. Alum

PAM® Cooking Spray
Yaley™ Gel Wax®
Yaley™ Brown Concentrated Candle Dye
Yaley™ White Concentrated Candle Dye
Bulls Eye® Amber Shellac
Design Master® Glossy Wood Tone Spray
Wood Shavings
DAP® Alex Plus® Caulk

Tools

- 9" Pie Pan
- Rolling Pin
- Saucepan
- Candle Thermometer
- Knife

Figure 42.1: The salt dough crust in pie pan

212 desserts

Preheat oven to 350°F. Spray the pie plate with PAM® cooking spray. To make the salt dough, mix the dry ingredients in a saucepan. Add water and vegetable oil. Heat over low heat until it is the consistency of mashed potatoes, stirring until there are no more clumps. Using a plastic spoon, scoop it out on to a lightly floured surface. Knead it until it is smooth and thick. Make a ball. Use immediately or refrigerate in an airtight container. Using a rolling pin, roll dough out so it is less than ⅛" thick. Place the dough in pie plate, pressing it into the bottom. Press a spoon in the crust around the edge to create a scalloped edge. Bake at 350°F for 25 minutes. Once the crust has cooled, remove it from the tart pan and coat it with amber shellac to give it a golden brown color. Be sure to add a little more shellac to areas that would have browned more in the baking process.

Melt a 4" × 4" block of Gel Wax® in a saucepan on low heat to create the cream filling. When the wax is melted, add white and brown concentrated dye shavings to reach the desired color of the milky cream of coconut cream pie.

Figure 42.3: Tinted Gel Wax® in salt dough crust

Before pouring the wax into the crust, stir in wood shavings. The wood shavings resemble coconut in the cream filling. Pour the tinted Gel Wax® in cooled salt dough crust.

Figure 42.2: Gel Wax® with dye melting in pan

Figure 42.4: Wood shavings painted to look like toasted coconut

Chopping wood shavings into small flakes creates the toasted coconut topping. Place wood shavings on a surface for painting. Putting them on plastic is helpful so they don't stick after painting. Mix a little burnt sienna paint and water together in a spatter consistency. Varying the amount of water and paint when spattering will yield different shades of toasted coconut flakes.

Once the coconut pie filling has cooled, add a layer of Alex Plus® Caulk to the top. Spread the caulk using a knife to get an even layer. Dipping the knife in water will keep the caulk from sticking to it. Add the toasted coconut flakes while the caulk is still drying. To add more definition from the baking process, spray a little Design Master® Glossy Wood Tone around the edges of the piecrust. If you want to cut a slice out of the pie, wait until the caulk has dried at least 2 hours. You should be able to use a regular sharp knife to cut through the caulk, gel wax, and crust.

Figure 42.5: Completed pie

forty three

gelatin mold

Total Time: 6 hours

Why This Works—The gel candle wax is tintable and durable, and has a realistic weight for the end product. It is a low-density candle wax and is long lasting and odorless. Adding a dash of color from the Yaley™ concentrated candle dye to the wax tints the entire wax. All of Yaley's candle dyes are compatible with the gel wax. If the budget is an issue, there has been success in tinting the wax by using crayons.

Show Application—This recipe could be used in *Picnic* by William Inge or to create jelly molds or flummery for Charles Dickens's *A Christmas Carol*.

Safety Precautions

- Always read and follow all manufacturers' directions.
- Don't pour any wax down the drain.
- Never leave melting wax unattended.
- Use a thermometer to monitor the temperature of the wax.
  - Don't overheat the wax. It will melt around 130°F. The optimum temperature is between 160°F and 170°F. Heat to a maximum of 220°F.
- Keep the wax away from an open flame.
- Always use a potholder when handling a hot pot.
- Always keep an ABC fire extinguisher nearby.

Ingredients

Yaley™ Gel Wax®
Yaley™ Red Concentrated Candle Dye
DAP® Alex Plus® Caulk
Smooth-On® Universal® Mold Release Aerosol Spray

Tools

- Gelatin Mold
- Saucepan
- Candle Thermometer
- Cake Decorator Star Tip
- Quart or Gallon-size Plastic Storage Bag

Figure 43.2: Gel Wax® melting in pan

Spray gelatin mold pan with Universal® Mold Release. Melt a block of Gel Wax® and Crème Wax® in a saucepan on low heat. Add red concentrated dye shavings to reach the desired color of Jell-O. Check wax temperature with candle thermometer prior to pouring. When the wax is completely melted and the correct color, pour molten wax into a gelatin mold.

216 desserts

Figure 43.2: Gel Wax® with concentrated red candle dye

Figure 43.3: Spraying gelatin mold pan with Universal® Mold Release

Allow the wax to completely set. This usually takes between 3 and 4 hours depending on volume and heat of the wax when it was poured.

After the wax has cooled, invert a decorative plate over the top of the mold and carefully flip it over. Gently lift off the mold. Some of the tricks for unmolding a traditional gelatin salad might be helpful: moistening the serving platter before unmolding the gelatin allows you to slide it around a little so you can center it perfectly on the plate and dunking the mold in warm water for about 10 seconds will loosen it. (Don't use hot water, it will melt the wax.)

Use a bag with a cake decorator star tip to create the starbursts of whipped cream with Alex Plus® Caulk. You can use an actual pastry bag with a decorating tip or you can use a plastic sandwich bag, cut a corner of bag off, insert the star tip through the hole and tape it in place. Fill the bag with Alex Plus® Caulk. Make sure you get most of the air out of the bag, close the top of the bag, roll the top of the bag down so the force of piping doesn't explode the caulking out the top of the bag. Hold the tip perpendicular to the surface just above the surface, squeeze the bag—don't lift up. To make pointy-tipped stars, pull up as you release the pressure. You should get a nice point at the top.

gelatin mold **217**

Figure 43.4: Gel Wax® in gelatin mold

forty four
pineapple upside-down cake

Total Time: 4 hours

Why This Works—The benefits for using most Smooth-On® products are that no scale is necessary, it is a simple ratio by volume, and perfect for beginners. The low viscosity of the products offers easy mixing and pouring. Smooth-Cast® 320 is an ultra-low viscosity casting resin and will create virtually bubble-free castings. It is easy to mix, pour, and add colorant to the mixture. It is durable, paintable, and moisture resistant. It captures a tremendous amount of detail. It has an extremely fast curing time of 10 minutes. Smooth-Cast® 320 is off-white when it cures.

FlexFoam-iT!® III expands 15 times its initial volume. It rises and cures quickly to a solid flexible foam. It has a pot life of 35 seconds. FlexFoam-iT!® III is the lowest density foam and expands the most.

OOMOO® 25 is easy to use, an inexpensive silicone rubber, and cures at room temperature with little shrinkage. The two parts are different colors (Part A is pink, Part B is blue) that make it evident when it is has been stirred thoroughly. It is fairly resistant to tearing after de-molding through a series of casts.

The gel candle wax is tintable and durable, and has a realistic weight for the end product. It is a low-density candle wax that is long lasting and odorless. Adding a dash of color from the Yaley™ concentrated candle dye to the wax tints the entire wax. All of Yaley's candle dyes are compatible with the gel wax. If the budget is an issue, there has been success in tinting the wax by using crayons.

According the experts at Smooth-On®, when creating a mold from a model that is porous or organic, the model needs to be sealed with an acrylic spray like Krylon® Crystal Clear Acrylic to prevent failure in the mold process. After it has dried, Mann Ease Release® 200 needs to be applied. Ease Release® 200 is an excellent general-purpose release agent and should be used with silicone molds like OOMOO®.

The GOLD line of Montana™ Spray lacquer is a high-covering and quick-drying NC-acrylic lacquer. NC-Acrylic lacquer is a solvent-based lacquer of acrylic resin base combined with a nitrocellulose and alkyd resin. It dries fast because of the rapid evaporation time of the solvent. The BLACK and GOLD lines can be combined. However, Montana GOLD works better on porous surfaces and the Montana BLACK works well on non-porous surfaces. This information is more significant if you are going to be creating murals.

Safety Precautions

- Use gloves and safety glasses when working with Smooth-On® products.
    - Use in a well-ventilated area and avoid directly inhaling mixing agents.
    - As Smooth-Cast® 320 cures, it will have visible fumes and the castings will be extremely hot.
    - Castings will reach full cure after 4–6 hours at room temperature.
- Always read and follow all manufacturers' directions.
- Don't pour any wax down the drain.
- Never leave melting wax unattended.
- Use a thermometer to monitor the temperature of the wax.
    - Don't overheat the wax. It will melt around 130°F. The optimum temperature is between 160°F and 170°F. Heat to a maximum of 220°F.
- Keep the wax away from an open flame.
- Always use a potholder when handling a hot pot.
- Always keep an ABC fire extinguisher nearby.
- Read and follow all manufacturers instructions.

Ingredients

Smooth-On® FlexFoam-iT!® III
Smooth-On® Universal® Mold Release Aerosol Spray and Ease Release® 2831
Dried Pineapple Pieces, 2
Krylon® Crystal Clear Acrylic Spray
Smooth-On® OOMOO® 25
Smooth-On® Smooth-Cast® 320
Smooth-On® Silc Pig® Yellow Concentrated Pigment for Silicone
Crayola® Model Magic®, white
Acrylic Paints
Yaley™ Gel Wax®
Yaley™ Red Concentrated Candle Dye
Bulls Eye® Amber Shellac
Montana™ GOLD Spray Paint in Smash Potato
Design Master® Glossy Wood Tone Spray

Tools

- 9" Cake Pan
- Foam-core board to create a box
- Plastic 8 oz. cup (a larger cup leaves room to stir)
- Small Artist Paint Brushes
- Hot Glue Gun

Figure 44.1: Finished FlexFoam-iT!® III cake base

The cake is created by using Smooth-On® FlexFoam-iT!® III. Spray the cake pan with Smooth-On® Universal® Mold Release aerosol spray followed by Ease Release® 2831. Let dry for 10 minutes. According to the Smooth-On® website, they caution against using the Universal® Mold Release by itself because it has been known to collapse the foam. They suggest lightly applying the release agent with a soft brush over all surfaces and letting it dry for 30 minutes. Smooth-On® FlexFoam-iT!® III is a two-part foam. Mix the parts by volume. Measure 1 part Part A and 2 parts Part B into separate plastic containers. The website suggests pre-mixing Part B with a mechanical mixer or drill before adding Part A *into* Part B. Mix for 30 seconds before pouring. Pour into 9" cake pan. The foam will completely set in 2 hours.

In a well-ventilated area or under a spray hood, use a light-yellow spray paint like Montana™ GOLD Smash Potato to give the cake its color. When this recipe was created, Montana™ had the color Smash Potato in the GOLD line. It has since been discontinued. It is available in the BLACK line (Smash 137's Potato)' or the Vanilla in the GOLD line could be substituted. To add more details from the baking process, spray Design Master® Glossy Wood Tone around the edges of the cake where the cake would brown against the pan.

Create a mold box by cutting foam-core board into one piece approximately 6" x 6" for the bottom and four pieces approximately 2" x 6". Hot glue the pieces together as an open-top box. The box should be 1" to 2" larger than two rings of dried pineapple. Hot glue two dried pineapple rings

Figure 44.2: Creating pineapple negative mold

Figure 44.3: Casting pineapple rings with Smooth-Cast® 320

to the bottom of mold box. It is important to glue the object firmly in place before making the mold. The silicone rubber of OOMOO® 25 will create a negative mold of the pineapple rings. Fill half of an 8 oz. plastic cup with Part A. Pour 4 oz. of Part B into the cup with Part A, which should fill the cup. You will have 8 oz. of product that will need to be combined. Using a larger graduated mixing container that is larger than 8 oz. will give you room to mix the two parts. Stir until the pink and blue liquids turn purple. You will only have 15 minutes to work with this. Pour the OOMOO® 25 into the mold box at the lowest point and cover the pineapple completely. Allow the OOMOO® 25 to set for 75 minutes.

To remove the mold from the mold box, cut along the hot-glued corners. Carefully, remove the pineapple rings from the mold. Smooth-Cast® 320 will be used to create the positive pineapple rings. It uses equal parts of Part A and Part B. Pour 4 oz. of Part A into a mixing plastic mixing container, followed by 4 oz. of Part B. Add a drop of yellow Silc Pig®. Silc Pig® is concentrated silicone color pigment. A little goes a long way. Stir thoroughly. You will only have 3 minutes to work with this. Pour the liquid into the mold. The pineapple rings will be ready to be removed from the mold in 15 minutes. Be careful when removing them from the mold, as the Smooth-Cast® 320 generates heat as it cures.

The cherries are made by rolling 1" x 1" cubes of Crayola® Model Magic® into balls. Stab a mechanical pencil into the center of the ball to create the depression where the stem and stone would have been. White Crayola® Model Magic® was used when this recipe was created. Crayola® Model Magic® does come in a variety of colors including red. If you had to make a lot of cherries you could start with the red Crayola® Model Magic® to speed up the painting process. Paint the cherries with a series of medium-red and red-orange acrylic paints to match research images.

Figure 44.4: Model Magic® formed into cherries

Place cake on serving plate. Attach the pineapple rings and cherries to the top of the cake with melted Gel Wax®. Melt a small 2″ x 2″ cube of Yaley™ Gel Wax® in a saucepan on low heat for the brown sugar sauce on top of the cake. Add a small amount of brown concentrated candle dye to the Gel Wax®. Brush amber shellac around the edges of the pineapple rings and cherries to replicate the caramelization that would happen during the baking process. Pour the brown sugar sauce over the cake. Let cool.

companion website information

On the companion website www.routledge.com/cw/honesty, there are many step-by-step fake food recipes, photos, and edible recipes that wouldn't fit within the pages of this book.

- Fruit Tray Appetizer
- Poppy Seed Muffins
- Beef Flank Steaks with Risotto
- General Tso's or Sesame Chinese Chicken with Fried Rice
- Large Christmas Goose
- Mini Berry Pies
- Edible Prop Foods
    - Beer
        - Pourable Pitcher
        - Bottle
    - Wines
        - Champagne
        - Chianti
        - White
    - Liquors, Liqueurs, and Aperitifs
        - Brandy
        - Campari®
        - Irish Cream
        - Pimm's® and Pimm's® Lemonade
        - Tawny Port
        - Irish Whiskey
        - Scotch Whisky
    - Miscellaneous
        - Coco-Cola®
        - Pepto Bismol™
        - Raspberry Sorbet that doesn't melt onstage
        - Edible Blood
        - Any many more

Also, there are links to helpful resources on the web for how-to videos and product information. Safety Data Sheets for all* the products used in this book are available on the companion website.

   If there are SDS sheets missing, it is purely an unintentional oversight.

helpful resources

- Color theory video: www.youtube.com/watch?v=WYZWDEmLR90
- How to make pierogi: https://en.wikipedia.org/wiki/Pierogi
- How to hold a piping bag: www.wilton.com/how-to-hold-a-piping-bag/WLTECH-391.html#sz=30&start=7
- Video on how to make stars, shells, spirals, and roses with a piping bag: www.youtube.com/watch?v=u59e2ImjoMg
- How to make a rope of icing: www.wilton.com/buttercream-rope/WLTECH-127.html
- How to choose the correct chemical resistant gloves: www.ansellpro.com/download/Ansell_7thEditionChemicalResistanceGuide.pdf and www.grainger.com/content/qt-166-chemical-resistance-gloves
- Hart, Eric. *Prop Building Guidebook: For Theatre, Film, and TV* (2nd ed.). New York: Routledge, 2017.

products used

- Rosco®: www.rosco.com
- Sculptural Arts Coating, Inc.: www.sculpturalarts.com
- Smooth-On®: www.smooth-on.com
- Smooth-On® Tutorials for Molding and Casting: www.smooth-on.com/tutorials/
- Rosco® Spectrum Blog: www.rosco.com/spectrum/
- Thai Unryu Paper: www.mulberrypaperandmore.com/c-247-unryu-paper.aspx

bibliography

"3M™ Fastbond™ Contact Adhesive 30NF." 3M™ United States, 2017. Web: www.3m.com/3M/en_US/company-us/all-3m-products/~/3M-Fastbond-Contact-Adhesive-30NF?N=5002385+3293241327&rt=rud.

"3M™ Super 77™ Multipurpose Spray Adhesive." 3M™ United States, n.d. Web: www.3m.com/3M/en_US/company-us/all-3m-products/~/3M-Super-77-Multipurpose-Spray-Adhesive?N=5002385+3293242460&rt=rud.

"Bulls Eye® Shellac." Zinsser® Bulls Eye® Shellac Product Page. Rustoleum®, 2013. Web: www.rustoleum.com/product-catalog/consumer-brands/zinsser/interior-wood-finishes/bulls-eye-shellac/.

"Creative Paperclay® Product." Creative Paperclay Co. - Air Hardening Modeling Materials for Artists & Crafters. Creative Paperclay®, n.d. Web: www.paperclay.com/product.htm.

Davis, Janice. "How to Make Salt Dough?" Learning 4 Kids, December 9, 2012. n.d. Web: www.learning4kids.net/2012/12/09/how-to-make-salt-dough-recipe/.

Dow Building Solutions. The Dow Chemical Company, 1995–2017. Web: http://building.dow.com/ap/en/.

FirstPalette.com. "Salt Dough." First Palette Kids' Crafts. N.p., n.d. Web: www.firstpalette.com/tool_box/art_recipes/Salt_Dough/Salt_Dough.html.

Foam Coatings, Clear Coats, Primers, Saturated Paints, Scenic Brushes by Sculptural Arts Coating, Inc. Sculptural Arts Coating, Inc., n.d. Web: www.sculpturalarts.com/.

Hacker, Richard Carleton. "Six of the Best Tawny Ports Available Today." Robb Report® Media, LLC, January 23, 2015. Web: http://robbreport.com/wine-spirits-cigars/slideshow/six-best-tawny-ports-available-today.

Krylon®: Make It Yours®. Krylon Products Group, February 1, 2017. Web: www.krylon.com/products/crystal-clear-acrylic/.

"Polly Plastics Moldable Plastics." Polly Plastics, 2017. Web: https://pollyplastics.com/collections/moldable-plastic.

"The Oyster and Its Origins." France Naissain, n.d. Web: www.francenaissain.com/en/the-oyster/the-oyster-and-its-origins/.

Rosco. N.d. Web: http://us.rosco.com/.

Tamaki, Leanne, and New Zealand Ministry for Culture and Heritage Te Manatu Taonga. "Pacific Oyster." Te Ara Encyclopedia of New Zealand. Ministry for Culture and Heritage Te Manatu Taonga, July 9, 2013. Web: www.teara.govt.nz/en/photograph/8023/pacific-oyster.

Titebond®. Franklin International, 2011. Web: www.titebond.com/Libraries/LiteraturePDFs/TT-683_GlueGuideTB.sflb.ashx.

"Unryu Paper." Light Weight Unryu Paper (Mulberry Paper). Mulberry Paper Design and More, n.d. Web: www.mulberrypaperandmore.com/c-247-unryu-paper.aspx.

Warren, Anna. "Finger Lickin' Good: Fried Chicken." Fake 'n Bake. N.p., October 17, 2012. Web: http://fake-n-bake.blogspot.com/2012_10_01_archive.html.

Index

*Note to index: Page numbers printed in **bold** refer to illustrative material.*

3M™ Fastbond™ Contact Adhesive 30NF 14, **14,** 95, 130, 195, 196, 207

acrylic medium 88
acrylic paints 9, 27, 29, 160, 178 *see also* Artist's Choice Saturated Scenic Paints™; Off Broadway™; Supersaturated™ Scenic Paints; Valspar® paints
adhesive spreader 11, **12**
adhesives 8, 11, 94, 95, 96; aerosol 157, 195; contact adhesive 14, **14,** 29 *see also* 3M™ Fastbond™ Contact Adhesive 30NF; DAP® Weldwood® Contact Cement; Elmer's® Glue-All®; Titebond® Wood Glue
Alex Plus® caulk 13, **13,** 34, **34,** 74, **74,** 84, **84,** 213, 216–17
almonds 151
apple tart 22, **189,** 190–3, **191, 192, 193**
Artist's Choice Saturated Scenic Paints™ 16, **16**

backer rod 128
bacon **79,** 83–4, **84;** for club sandwich 121, **121**
baguette 26, 27, **27**
baked potato with butter and sour cream **93,** 94–7, **96, 97**
band saw 14
barbecue ribs with corn on the cob **99,** 100–5, **104, 105**
beans (green) 61, **61**
beer **165,** 165–7, **167**
beverages: beer **165,** 165–7, **167;** hot chocolate **168,** 169–70; Irish coffee **171,** 172–3; lemonade **174,** 175–6; martini with olives **177,** 178–80; milk **181,** 182–3; orange juice **183;** piña colada 184, **184**
Bounty® paper towels *see* paper products

bread **25,** 26–31; baguette 26, 27, **27;** club sandwich **117,** 118–22, **120, 122;** rustic round 26, **27,** 29; rye loaf 29–31, **30;** sourdough bread 26, 28, **28**
breakfast foods: bacon **79,** 83–4, **84;** doughnuts **71,** 72–4, **73, 74, 75;** eggs (over easy/fried) **79,** 80–1, **81;** oatmeal muffins **76, 77,** 77–8, **78;** pancakes **79, 82,** 82–3, **83**
Brie cheese 33–5, **34, 35**
broccoli **62,** 62–3
Bulls Eye® Shellac 12, 27, 28, 29, 31, 143, 173, 197
buns (sticky) *see* sticky buns
butter 97, **97**

cake with removable piece **194,** 195–9, **198, 199, 200**
candle beads (soy) 89, **89**
candle dyes 12; cheese 33, 34, 36, 98, 110; gelatin mold **216;** hot chocolate 169; shrimp cocktail 55, 57; tomatoes 151
candle wax *see* candle beads (soy); crème candle wax; gel candle wax
candle wax thermometer 11, **12**
caramel drizzle 193, **193**
carrots 61, **61**
casting 17, **40, 56;** lobster meat **140;** pineapple rings 221, **221;** wax **102,** 102–3 *see also* mold-making; OOMOO® 25; OOMOO® 30; Smooth-Cast® 300; Smooth-Cast® 320
caulk *see* Alex Plus® caulk
Cheddar cheese 33, 35
cheese: Brie 33–5, **34, 35;** Cheddar cheese 33, 35; Gouda cheese 33, 36, **36;** grated/shredded 98, **98,** 107, 110, **110;** platter **32, 36;** Swiss cheese 33, **35,** 36, **36**
cheese grater 10

chef salad **106,** 107–8, **111**; cheese 107, 110, **110**; eggs 107, 111, **111**; lettuce 107, **108,** 108–9, **109**; meat 107, 109, **109**; tomatoes 107, 109, **110**
cherries 221, **222**
cherry pie **201,** 202–4, **203, 204**
cherry tomatoes *see* tomatoes
chicken lo mein **112,** 113–15, **115**
chicken wings **37,** 37–40, **39, 40, 41**
Chinese food **42,** 43–6; chicken lo mein **112,** 113–15, **115**; egg rolls **42,** 43–4, **44**; soy sauce **42,** 45–6, **46**; spring rolls **42,** 44–5, **45**; wonton soup **64,** 65–7, **66, 67, 68**; filling **66**
chocolate cake à la mode **205, 206,** 206–9, **209**
chocolate milk **182**
clamps 10–11, 126
club sandwich **117,** 118–22, **120, 122**
coatings 14–15, 16
coconut **212,** 212–13
coconut cream pie **210,** 211–13, **212, 213**
color pigments 18
cookie cutters 10
corn on the cob **99,** 100–2, **101, 102**
Crayola® Model Magic® 8, **113, 114,** 139, 140, 209, **209**; apple slices 191, **192**; cherries 221, **222**; hard-boiled eggs 111; hot chocolate 169; marshmallows **170**; olives **178,** 179; vegetable tray 60
Creative Paperclay® 43–4, **149,** 149–50
crème candle wax **13,** 33, 94, 98, **98,** 100, 102, **102**; Cheddar cheese 35–6; cheese platter 34; cherry pie 203; diced tomatoes 151; gelatin mold 215–16; spinach quiche 153
CrystalGel® 15, **15,** 62, 74, 131, 134–5, 146, 209; icing 197, 207; lettuce 107, 108–9, 134, **134,** 135, 151; mayonnaise **121,** 121–2
cutting mats 8
cutting tools 7–8, 10, 14

DAP® Weldwood® Contact Cement 14
decorating tools 11
Design Master® paints 12; *see also* Glossy Wood Tone Spray

desserts: apple tart **189,** 190–1, **191, 192, 193**; cherry pie **201,** 202–4; chocolate cake à la mode **205, 206,** 206–9, **209**; coconut cream pie **210,** 211–13, **212, 213**; gelatin mold **214,** 215–17; pineapple upside-down cake **218,** 219–20
doughnuts **71,** 72–4, **73, 74, 75**
Dragon Skin®10 Fast 86–8, **87**
Dremel® tool 14, **95,** 104
dyeing 113, 114–15, **115** *see also* candle dyes

Ease Release® 17, **17**
egg rolls **42,** 43–4, **44**
eggs: hard-boiled 107, 111, **111**; over easy/fried **79,** 80–1, **81**
Elmer's® Glue-All® 8–9, 11, 94, 190
Encapso® K 17, **17,** 65, 67, **68, 176**; lemonade **175,** 175–6; martini with olives 178–80, **179, 180**; milk 182–3; piña colada 185, **185, 186**
Ethafoam® 124

fabrics: club sandwich 119, **119**
FlexBond™ 15, **15,** 52, 66, **96,** 195
FlexCoat™ 15, **15,** 27, 28, 29, 128
FlexFoam-iT!® III 18, **18,** 80; bread 26, 29, **29,** 30; doughnuts **72,** 72–3, **73, 74**; eggs **81,** 81–2; pancakes **82,** 82–3; pineapple upside-down cake 219, 220
FlexFoam-iT!®-V 167; doughnuts 72–3; hot chocolate **167**; Irish coffee **173**; oatmeal muffins **77,** 77–8, **78**; piña colada 185–6, **186**; sticky buns 86, 87, 88, **88**
flexible polyurethane foam (FPF) 12, **13,** 18, 119, **119, 120**
foam *see* flexible polyurethane foam (FPF); rigid extruded polystyrene (XPS)
FoamCoat® 15, **15**
French enamel varnish (FEV) 84, 131, 160
frosting *see* icing

gel candle wax **13,** 33, 55, 80, 94, 107, 118; beer **166,** 166–7; caramel drizzle **193**; Cheddar cheese 35–6; cheese platter 34, **34**; cherry pie 202–4, **203**; cocktail sauce 57; coconut

cream pie 212, **212**; coloring **121**; diced tomatoes 151, **151**; eggs 81–2, 111; gelatin mold **215**, 215–16, **216**; gravy 147; hot chocolate 169, **169**; Irish coffee 172, **172,** 173; melting **120**; pineapple upside-down cake 219, 222; safety precautions 33, 80; soy sauce 46; spinach quiche 153, **154,** 154–5; syrup 83
gelatin mold **214,** 215–17
glazes 130, 157
Glossy Wood Tone® Spray 12, **13,** 27, 28, **28,** 131, 220; apple tart 192; cheese 36; cherry pie 204; coconut cream pie **213**; lettuce leaves 151; turkey 161
Gouda cheese 33, 36, **36**
grated/shredded cheese 98, **98**
gravy 147, **147**
green beans *see* beans (green)

ham **129,** 130–1, **131, 132**
hanging meat *see* meat
hot chocolate **168,** 169–70
hot glue guns 8

ice cream 208, **208**
icing **197,** 197–200, **198, 199, 200, 207,** 207–8, **208**
India ink 12, **52**; noodles 114–15
Irish coffee **171,** 172–3

Japanese Ryoba Saw 10, **10,** 125–7, 130, 158

Kangaroo® Liquid Latex 126
knives 7, 8

latex (liquid) **14,** 14–15, 48–9, 126; honey-glazed ham 131, **131**; turkey 160, **160**
lemonade **174,** 175–6
lettuce 62, **63,** 107, **108,** 108–9, **109**; for club sandwich **120**; side salad 150, **150**; wraps **133,** 134–5, **135, 136**
Liquitex® String Gel 175
lobster tail **137, 138,** 138–40, **139, 140**

Mann Ease Release® 17, **18**
marking utensils 7
marshmallows **170**
martini with olives **177, 178,** 178–80, **180**
mashed potato 146
mayonnaise 121, **121**
measuring tools 7, 11
meat: filling for lettuce wraps 135, **135**; hanging **123,** 124–6; honey-glazed ham **129,** 130–1, **131, 132**; peppered salami **127,** 127–8; roast beef **144, 146, 147**; in salad 107, 109, **109**; salami **125,** 125–6, **126**; sausage 128, **128**; turkey **156, 158, 159, 160, 161**
meat netting 124, 126, **126**
milk **181, 182,** 182–3
Minwax® wood stains 128, 160
mixing containers 9
mixing tools 9–10
modeling clay 8
mold boxes 38–9, **56,** 87, **101,** 101–2, 103, 220–1
mold-making 38–9; positive models 138; products 17, 38, 39 (*see also* OOMOO® 25; OOMOO® 30); tutorials 5 *see also* negative molds
mold release 17–18, 26, 35, 36, 38, 55, 77
Montana™ spray paints 82, 83, 219, 220
muffins: oatmeal **76, 77,** 77–8, **78**

NC-Acrylic lacquer 80
negative molds 39, 56, **102,** 103, **104**
noodles: chicken lo mein **112, 114,** 114–15
nuts: almonds 151

oatmeal muffins **76, 77,** 77–8, **78**
Off Broadway™ 15–16, **16,** 29, 61, 62, 63, 125, 126, 128; lobster tail 135–6, 139, 140; roast beef 146–7
olives **178,** 179, **179, 180**
OOMOO® 25 55, **56**; pineapple upside-down cake 219, 221
OOMOO® 30 17, **18,** 38, 39, **103**; barbecue ribs 100, 101–2, 104

orange juice **183**
orbital sander 10
oysters on half shell **47, 48,** 48–9, **49**

packing peanuts 51–2, **52,** 135
paint brushes 9, **9**
paints 15–16; acrylic paints 9, 27, 29, 160, 178; Design Master® paints 12 *see also* Artist's Choice Saturated Scenic Paints™; Glossy Wood Tone Spray; Montana™ spray paints; Off Broadway™; Supersaturated™ Scenic Paints
pancakes **79, 82,** 82–3, **83**
paper products 9; paper towels 9, 62–3, **63, 134,** 134–5; Thai Unryu paper 45, 67, 116, 154, **154**; tissue 107
papier-mâché 160, **160**
pellets (plastic) *see* plastic pellets
personal protection equipment (PPE) 19
pierogi **141, 142,** 142–3, **143**
piña colada 184, **184**
pineapple rings **221**
pineapple upside-down cake **218,** 219–22, **220**
planes *see* Surform®
plastic pellets 12, **13,** 83, 94, 97, **97**
plastic sheeting 84, **84**
Polly Plastics™ Moldable Plastic Pellets *see* plastic pellets
popcorn **50, 51,** 51–3, **52, 53**
positive models 138
potatoes: baked potato with butter and sour cream **93,** 94–7, **96, 97**; mashed 146
Premiere Clear Water Based Polyurethane Gloss 16, **17,** 28, 41, 161, 179

rasps *see* Surform®
rigid extruded polystyrene (XPS) 13, **13**; apple tart **190,** 191–2, **192**; baked potato 94–7, **96**; barbecue ribs 104; bread 26–8; cake 195, 196, **196**; chocolate cake à la mode **206,** 206–7, **207**; honey-glazed ham **130,** 130–1; laminating 26, 157–9, **158,** 195; peppered salami 127–8; roast beef 145–6, **146**; salami 125, 126; turkey 157–9, **158, 159**

roast beef with mashed potato and gravy **144,** 145–6, **146, 147**
Rosco® Labs *see* CrystalGel; FlexBond™; FlexCoat™; FoamCoat; Off Broadway™; Premiere Clear; Supersaturated™ Scenic Paints
rubber 17, 65
rustic round (bread) 26, **27,** 29
rye bread 26, 29–31, **30**

Safety Data Sheets (SDS) 19
safety equipment 19
safety precautions 38, 55
salad: side salad **148,** 150, **150, 151** *see also* chef salad
salami **125,** 125–6, **126**; peppered 127, **127**
salmon fillet with side salad **148, 149,** 149–50, **150, 151**
salt dough 8, **43,** 145; apple tart 190, 191, **191, 192**; cherry pie 202–4, **204**; coconut cream pie **211,** 211–12, **212**; egg rolls 43–4; mashed potato 146–7, **147**; pierogi **142,** 142–3, **143**; recipes 21–2; spinach quiche **153,** 153–5, **154**; storing 22; wonton soup 65–7, **66, 67**
sandpaper 9
saws 10, **10,** 14, 131
Sculpt or Coat® 15, 48–9, **49,** 150
Sculptural Arts Coating, Inc. *see* Artist's Choice Saturated Scenic Paints™; Sculpt or Coat®
sealers 16, **41,** 56, 125–6, 161
shellac 12, 78, 84, 88, 150, 212; amber **44,** 44–5, 78, 81–2, 88, 154–5, 167, 191–2, 203, **203,** 204, 222; beer 167; for French enamel varnish (FEV) 84, 131, 160 *see also* Bulls Eye® Shellac
shrimp cocktail **54,** 55–8, **56, 57, 58**; cocktail sauce **57,** 57–8
Silc Pig® 18, **18,** 29, **30,** 104, 182, 183, 186, **186,** 221
silicone color pigment *see* Silc Pig®
silicone rubber *see* Dragon Skin®10 Fast; OOMOO® 25; OOMOO® 30
Smooth-Cast® 300 18, **18,** 39–41, **40,** 56–7; barbecue ribs 100, 104, **104**
Smooth-Cast® 320 219, 221, **221**

Smooth-On® *see* Dragon Skin®10 Fast; Encapso® K; FlexFoam-iT!® III; Mann Ease Release®; OOMOO® 25; OOMOO® 30; Silc Pig®; Smooth-Cast® 300; Smooth-Cast® 320; Universal® mold release; Universal® Mold Release
soups: wonton soup **64**
sour cream 97, **97**
sourdough bread 26, 28, **28**
soy sauce **42,** 45–6, **46**
spatulas 9–10, **10**
spinach 154
spinach quiche **152, 153, 154, 155**
spring rolls **42,** 44–5, **45**
sticky buns **85, 87,** 87–9, **88, 89**
Supersaturated™ Scenic Paints 15–16; baked potato 96, 97; cake with removeable piece 196; chocolate cake à la mode 207; club sandwich 121; honey-glazed ham 132; martini with olives 179; pierogi 143
Surform® 10, **11,** 27, 28, 29, 158, 159
Swiss cheese 33, **35,** 36, **36**

tarts: apple tart 22, **189,** 190–1, **191, 192, 193**; spinach quiche **153,** 153–5, **154, 155**
Thai Unryu paper 45, 67, 116, 154, **154**
Titebond® Wood Glue 11, **11,** 27, 28, 126, 127, 158–9, 196

tomatoes **60,** 61, **61,** 107, 109, **110**; for club sandwich 120, **121**; diced **151**
tools: cutting tools 7–8, **8,** 10, 14; decorating tools 11–12; measuring tools 7, 11
turkey **156,** 157–9, **158, 159, 160, 161**
tweezers 10

Universal® Mold Release 17, **18,** 34, 35, 36, 72, 151, **216,** 220
upholstery foam *see* flexible polyurethane foam (FPF)

Valspar® paints 28, 29, 160
vegetable tray **59,** 60–3; broccoli **62,** 62–3; carrots **61**; lettuce 62, **63**; tomatoes **61**

wonton soup **64,** 65–7, **66, 67, 68**
wood stains 128

X-acto® knives 7, **7**
XPS *see* rigid extruded polystyrene (XPS)

Yaley™ *see* crème candle wax; gel candle wax

Zinsser® *see* Bulls Eye® Shellac